"I can't afford for my organization to be at less than 100 percent performance. As an engineer, I've leaned on the traditional quantitative methods. However, when organizations ail, these aren't much help. The Cohens' methods are. I highly recommend them and their book."

—William Rowley, Ph.D., President
Rowley International

"Many major businesses might still be around had someone in them read this book. The Cohens have developed a practical way of applying clinical psychology to organizations that anyone can use to diagnose and treat ailing firms, but well firms can greatly benefit also."

—Nancy Croft Baker, Senior Editor, *Environment Today*
co-author, *The Frugal Marketer*

"Must reading for change agents, consultants, and leaders at all levels of an organization. Should be a best seller."

—John Wholihan, Dean, College of Business Administration
Loyola Marymount University

"A ground-breaking approach, guaranteed to stimulate new ideas, new perceptions of problems and new approaches to problem-solving."

—Cort Durocher, Executive Director
American Institute of Aeronautics and Astronautics

"A very prgamatic approach to understanding and treating psychotic and neurotic illnesses affecting our organizations."

—Esker Davis
The Jet Propulsion Laboratory

"An eye-opener which charts new courses in understanding and treating organizational illnesses...a fresh and practical approach."

—Marlene W. Futterman, Executive Director
Direct Selling Educational Foundation

"Brilliant.... Clearly one of the most important books to appear this year....Indispensable for managers and entrepreneurs."

—Richard Poe, former Senior Editor, *Success Magazine*
author, *How to Profit from the Coming Russian Boom*

THE
PARANOID
CORPORATION
AND 8 OTHER WAYS
YOUR COMPANY
CAN BE CRAZY

*Advice From
an Organizational Shrink*

THE
PARANOID
CORPORATION
AND 8 OTHER WAYS
YOUR COMPANY
CAN BE CRAZY

Advice From
an Organizational Shrink

William A. Cohen, Ph.D. ◆ Nurit Cohen, Ph.D.

amacom

American Management Association

New York • Atlanta • Boston • Chicago • Kansas City • San Francisco • Washington, D.C.
Brussels • Toronto • Mexico City

Library of Congress Cataloging-in-Publication Data

Cohen, William A., 1937–
     The paranoid corporation and 8 other ways your company can
be crazy : advice from an organizational shrink / William A.
Cohen. Nurit Cohen.
     p.   cm.
     Includes bibliographical references and index.
     ISBN 0-8144-5129-2 : $22.95
     1. Management—Psychological   aspects.   2.   Corporate
turnarounds—Psychological aspects.   3. psychology, Industrial.
     4. Psychoanalysis. I. Cohen, Nurit, 1944- . II. Title.
III. Title: Paranoid corporation and eight other ways your
company can be crazy.
     HD38.C573   1993
     658'.001"9—dc20   93-24142
                                                        CIP

Printing number

10 9 8 7 6 5 4 3 2 1

Contents

Introduction

Psychology and Business: Art Meets Science

For many years the two authors of this book have shared a professional relationship in addition to a marital one. One of us has a background in corporate and military management and has been a business professor for many years. The other is a psychologist with both a clinical and an organizational degree. About fifteen years ago we began to combine our talents to help executives in industry and government to achieve more of their potential.

At about the same time, Americans suddenly "discovered" the quality techniques that had led to such stunning success in Japanese companies, and troubled U.S. corporations began racing one another to implement these new methods. In their rush toward excellence, business leaders often did not stop to consider what their specific problem was, and whether the quality techniques would make a difference; "quality" was seen as a kind of magic pill that would cure all problems.

In the course of our research and consulting work over the next few years, we began to observe that these quality methods didn't always work, no matter how skillfully they were applied. We also found that while they did indeed help some companies, they left others worse off.

Now, any psychologist knows that when it comes to

human patients, using the same treatment for all disorders is ridiculous. No single treatment can work for all psychological problems; what is worse, using the wrong treatment can actually cause harm. And we began to wonder whether that could also be said of organizations.

That line of thinking eventually led us to the ideas that are presented in this book:

- That organizations have distinct personalities, just like people
- That organizations can become psychologically sick, just like people
- That just like human patients, sick organizations can be made well again using treatments taken from clinical psychology

Psychoanalysis for business is not new. Consultants began using analytical techniques with businesses in the early 1980s. However, this idea is very difficult to apply in practice. One major problem is time.

Classical psychoanalysis requires the patient to gain insight. It is not a question of simply telling patients what is wrong. In order for psychoanalysis to be helpful, patients must reach real insight into their problems more or less on their own. The psychologist simply leads the way. Human patients need this process; without it, the problem often returns. However, gaining insight can take years, literally, and few companies can afford the luxury of that much time. There is a very real potential for failure before the treatment can work.

There are other problems, too, with using psychoanalytic procedures with businesses. A serious stumbling block is that one needs training in psychology or psychiatry to render effective treatment. Therefore, to make clinical psychology practical for business, we needed another approach.

We turned to cognitive/behavioral therapy. This style of therapy is much faster, for it doesn't depend on a patient's developing insight. It permits us to construct "how to" treatments that any manager can use, because this type of therapy does not require special training. It does demand accurate diagnosis and quick action, and so we developed a nontechnical diagnostic survey and a set of treatment procedures that anyone can use.

Then we tried this new process with companies that had used other methods to solve their problems but had not been successful. The techniques proved extremely valuable. Using this new approach to organizational therapy, troubled companies began to recover.

Many of the techniques described in this book are familiar to psychologists. However, we have refined them so that individuals with little or no psychological background can easily use them.

To illustrate how a nonpsychologist can use these practical techniques, we have included a number of examples from the business world. Some of the companies involved are well-known and are identified by their real names; others have had their identities disguised. But all the examples represent actual events, and all can help you learn to recognize early warning signs of illness in your own organization. That knowledge will empower you to help your company.

This book won't turn you into a clinical psychologist. It won't give you a quick fix, or even a sure fix. Organizations are by definition complex, and business organizations exist in a world that is becoming more complicated every day. Much as we might like to see one, there is no magic pill for sick companies. What this book can do is help you understand what is happening in your organization and suggest real-world solutions that can help.

1

Breakthrough for Unwell Organizations

In individuals, insanity is rare, but in groups, parties, nations and epochs it is the rule.

—*Friedrich Nietzsche,* Beyond Good and Evil

The point of therapy is to get unhooked, not to thrash around on how you got hooked.

—*Marianne Walters, family therapist, in* Family Secrets

Have you ever been in an organization that took actions that made no sense? Have you ever worked in a company that made self-defeating decisions? Were you ever part of a group that seemed to be out of control, working at cross-purposes, and going in all directions at once, none of them very logical? And have you ever thought to yourself, "Why, that's just crazy"?

You may have been closer to the truth than you realized. Organizations, like people, have distinct personalities and—like people—sometimes get sick. When the organization's personality is sick, it infects the people within and around it. If allowed to go untreated, the illness can cause serious harm, even a complete breakdown.

Fortunately, just as people can be returned to health, so can companies. When the organizational personality is healthy, it gives its members an inoculation that helps ward off failure.

It creates a comfortable work atmosphere that empowers members to do their best.

How companies can be made well and how you can play a key role in that process constitute the focus of this book.

When an Organization Gets Sick

Our approach to improving dysfunctional companies rests on a concept from organizational theory: that an organization is its own entity, with its own personality, separate from the individual personalities of the people who make up the organization. To fully appreciate this, consider a brutal but undeniable example: the lynch mob. A mob is, in the pure sense, an organization. It has been established to perform a specific function. It has a leader. It has members who perform various roles and tasks in support of the general mission.

The individual people who make up the mob may well be rational, caring human beings. Every one of them, acting as individuals, would recoil from the gruesome mission that they, as the mob, carry out. But the particular combination of events and individual personalities produces a circumstance in which the whole is greater than the sum of the parts, and the mob becomes its own creature, with a life of its own.

That same phenomenon has been observed in the business world: individuals unable to explain irrational actions that they take while part of the organizational dynamic. Here is an example.

A large manufacturing company suffered major reverses. Company executives believed that the negligence of some managers—they weren't sure who—was the cause, and the president established an advisory committee to pinpoint those responsible. Before they were done, the committee members had fired or demoted more than a hundred managers, most of whom had little or nothing to do with the losses. Most of those terminated went on to highly successful positions with other companies, including competitors.

One who served on the advisory committee later said, "At

first it was difficult fixing blame. Then we found one or two managers that we thought were guilty. Before you knew it, we got carried away. It was like a sickness. I don't really know why or how we could have made such a mess of things and punished so many people, mostly without cause."

Again, the whole was greater than the sum of the parts. The committee took on its own personality, completely separate from the individuals in it.

If an organization can develop its own personality, it follows, then, that this organizational personality can become psychologically ill, just as human personalities can. In fact, as you will see later in this chapter, we can call these organizational illnesses by the same names as those given to human disorders. And we can treat these illnesses with the same methods as we use with human patients; we can, in effect, say that our "patient" is the whole organization.

Matching the Cure to the Sickness

Management experts have tried many ways to help troubled companies, with varying degrees of success. Two approaches popular in recent years are the total quality management concept borrowed from the Japanese and the traits of excellence described in the book *In Search of Excellence*. Sometimes these solutions worked only temporarily, sometimes not at all.

The authors of *In Search of Excellence* surveyed many companies and identified qualities that excellent organizations share. From this they suggested that managers needed to innovate, focus on their customers, and take care of their people. These simple ideas helped thousands of businesses. Yet only a few years later *Business Week* reported a surprising discovery. A significant number of the "excellent" companies were bankrupt or in serious trouble!

More recently, American managers, told to emulate the Japanese methods of total quality management, formed special teams to work on problems. Top management met regularly with employees "to really listen." Most experts expected significant gains through these methods. Some went so far as to say that total quality management was the answer to all of a company's problems.

It wasn't. In 1991, *Fortune* magazine described a two-part survey in which 750,000 middle managers from one thousand large companies were asked over two three-year periods (1985–87 and 1988–90) to rank how their organizations were doing on several issues that a total quality program could be expected to improve. Between the first survey and the second, *fewer* managers said that their companies' executives communicated well with employees and listened to their problems; *fewer* said that companies treated them with respect as individuals; and *fewer* said that the company was a good place to work.[1]

Want more evidence? Florida Power & Light, winner of Japan's Deming Prize for quality management, gutted its quality program. Why? The workers were complaining. The Wallace Company, a Houston oil supply company, won the prestigious Malcolm Baldrige National Quality Award. Shortly afterward, it filed for protection under the Chapter 11 bankruptcy law.[2]

What's wrong with this picture? Should we conclude that quality programs are a waste of time? Should we burn our copies of *In Search of Excellence?* Of course not. Both these approaches are valuable; both can have a major impact on performance, quality of work life, and motivation. The problem is that they were being used by people with inappropriate expectations.

A quality program, no matter how well conceived, cannot cure an organization of its psychological illness, any more than an exercise program can cure a person of chicken pox. One has nothing to do with the other. The illness will overpower the other improvement efforts. When an organization is sick, it's sick. To cure it, you must get at the root of the problem.

    1. Anne B. Fisher, "Morale Crisis," *Fortune*, 18 November 1991, p. 70.
    2. Jay Mathews and Peter Katel, "The Cost of Quality," *Newsweek*, 7 September 1992, p. 48.

Treating the Disease, Not the Symptoms

When their organizations start to flounder, managers use a variety of methods and techniques to correct the problem. They invest a great deal of time, money, and energy, but things don't get better. In spite of hard work and goodwill on the part of everyone concerned, the problem persists.

The fatal error is trying to fix the surface situation without doing anything about the underlying psychological cause of the problem. To get at the root problem, you must treat the illness rather than the symptoms. And that requires you to view the whole organization as a patient.

Treating an organization as one patient rather than as a multitude of employees is a new concept on the cutting edge of psychology. This simple concept has these important advantages:

1. *It's the fastest way to turn things around.* Because individuals may react differently to the same basic problems, if you were to work on individual personalities you would have to treat many different symptoms. So even if temporarily successful, such a method can be dreadfully slow. In contrast, treating the fundamental illness has an immediate impact and causes rapid improvement.
2. *It enables you to uncover the real problem.* If you treat only the surface symptoms, the organization, like any patient, may feel better temporarily, but it remains sick. Eventually the sickness will overwhelm any temporary improvement. Treating only symptoms can often make the situation worse, for the treatment may mask other problems.
3. *It allows you to pursue effective treatment.* Working with the organization as a whole, you're far more likely to make the right diagnosis. And you can't begin the right treatment until you make the right diagnosis. The wrong medicine can be more dangerous than the illness itself because it can easily make the disease worse.

The Nine Psychological Disorders

There are nine major organizational diseases, and they are all very serious.

- They destroy employee morale.
- They rob the company of productivity.
- They contribute to low-quality products.
- They hurt customers.
- They frustrate and damage the careers and peace of mind of both rank-and-file employees and top management.
- They cause companies to take illogical, crazy actions.
- They make improvement in quality almost irrelevant.
- They have the potential for destroying leadership and wrecking any organization.

However, while their impact is almost always grave, these ailments are all different. They cause different types of problems and manifest different symptoms. They require different treatment. So a basic understanding of these different diseases is the first step.

In labeling these organizational illnesses, we used the same nomenclature as used for human psychology, on the assumption that the names are at least somewhat familiar to most people. Continuing this parallel with human illnesses, we then grouped the diseases into two broad categories: psychoses and neuroses.

Psychologists define a psychosis as an illness in which contact with reality is lost. A psychotic company incorrectly rates its own perceptions and makes incorrect inferences about what is going on outside, even in the face of clear evidence to the contrary. Neuroses are emotional disorders that, while not divorced from reality, can nonetheless be disabling. Neurotic organizations display anxiety, fear, and an irrational focus on avoiding the negative rather than working toward the positive. The individual illnesses break down into these categories in the following way:

Psychoses

- Manic behavior
- Manic-depression
- Schizophrenia
- Paranoia

Neuroses

- Neurotic behavior
- Depression
- Intoxication
- Obsessive compulsion
- Post-trauma syndrome

In the chapters ahead, each illness is described and discussed in detail.

Helping Your Organization Get Well: An Overview

All kinds of organizations are subject to psychological illness: large corporations, small businesses, nonprofit agencies, government bodies, military units. The organization in question may be as mammoth as the largest multinational corporation, or as small as a four-person department. It may be a brand-new enterprise dealing with ultrasophisticated technology, or a traditional neighborhood business owned by the same family for three generations. No organization—no matter what size or type or industry—is immune.

That's the bad news. The good news is that all these illnesses can be cured, and it doesn't take a trained psychologist to do it. Using the techniques presented in this book, anyone who sees a problem and cares enough to want to fix it can undertake a treatment program.

That bears repeating: Managers *at any level* can institute treatments for sick organizations. In a few cases, certain treatments that we suggest are best done by senior management. But it is by no means true that only the top executives of an organization can effect changes; in fact, sometimes they are the source of the problem and are blind to its insidious effects.

No matter where you are in the organization, you can treat the problem in your own little corner. It doesn't matter where the illness originated, or how widespread it is, or whether it takes different forms in other departments. All that matters is that in your own area, you make a commitment to treat the illness, and you take action.

And then a magical thing begins to happen. As your treatment plan starts to show results, your own department or division stands out from the rest of the organization like a shining light of rationality. That light breaks through the cracks in other departments, illuminating the corners and enabling other managers to see their situation in new ways. Soon they too are looking at treatment possibilities, asking you how you managed it, and developing their own plans.

Wellness is contagious, just like illness.

You may be eager to roll up your sleeves and start treating what you think you see around you. Resist that temptation until you understand the process; you could conceivably do more harm than good. Let's start first with an overview; then you can proceed intelligently and with understanding.

1. You start by examining your patient—the organization— and analyzing its organizational health. You do this by using a self-administered questionnaire that we developed: the Organizational Health Analyzer. It is built on sound diagnostic procedures but designed so that anyone can use it.
2. Because having the right diagnosis is absolutely critical, you then confirm your original diagnosis with some simple follow-up tests.
3. Next you develop a plan that outlines how you will go about treating the illness. We describe several possible treatments for each illness in the chapters that follow, and we show you how to plan an approach that makes sense for your particular situation.

4. Finally, you carry out your plan, monitoring the results and calling on backup ideas if the situation changes.
5. Along the way, you take steps to make sure you don't get swept up in the overall craziness that has infected your organization. Creating a "sphere of wellness" around yourself protects your own sanity and your ability to be effective.

The next nine chapters explain the nine organizational illnesses and describe treatment options for each. Chapter 11 shows you how to diagnose illness and confirm that diagnosis; Chapter 12 presents ways for you to create a sphere of wellness around yourself; and Chapter 13 takes you through the steps of creating and implementing a treatment plan. Chapter 14 ties the entire process together by recounting the experience of one manager who successfully cured his organization of a life-threatening illness.

2

"We're Going to the Moon!"— Manic Behavior

Madness need not be all breakdown. It may also be break-through. It is potential liberation and renewal as well as enslavement and existential death.

—R. D. Laing, The Divided Self

Watch an individual who is manic, and you might think you are looking at someone high on drugs. A manic person becomes intensely excited, talks fast, moves nervously, laughs too much, and makes grandiose plans that have no grounding in reality.

When an organization becomes manic, excessive enthusiasm sweeps away hardheaded business logic and common sense. A manic organization often has a long string of successes and comes to believe itself invincible. Soaring on a high of overconfidence, it spends more and more time on grand plans and pays less and less attention to the details that ensure success—or failure. Eventually, failure to take care of some critical detail brings everything crashing down.

A Tale of Manic Behavior

Some years ago, a small company in California came up with the idea of marketing premixed wine and fruit juice, the product that later came to be called the wine cooler. Market research was very positive, and taste tests of the mixes were favorable. Excitement grew. The company rushed feverishly ahead.

With extreme enthusiasm and confidence carrying it forward like a steamroller, the company searched for more capital. It sold investors on big investments and spent all the money it could get. After producing high-cost samples that used fruit juice and wine purchased from wholesalers, the company accelerated its efforts, buying more machinery, hiring additional personnel, and spending money in a grand way. It sold twenty thousand cases of the wine cooler even before the production line opened.

There was one small problem. The company was not in the spirits business. No one had bothered to look fully into the costs of the wine needed, and the company learned far too late that the taxes involved were 700 percent higher than its estimate. That meant it would be impossible to sell the product at an acceptable price. The line folded even before it got started, and it took the company with it.

Symptoms of manic behavior in organizations include the following:

- Expansive moods
- Grandiosity
- Excessive excitement
- Little attention paid to detail

Enthusiasm and confidence are not inherently wrong, as long as they are appropriately grounded in reality. It is when enthusiasm becomes excessive, and confidence ungrounded, that we must be wary.

The Danger of Unrealistic Enthusiasm

In 1988, EPI Products introduced to the American market a personal-care product called Epilady. This appliance enabled women to remove leg hair at home with results similar to those of wax treatments given in professional salons. Already a success in Europe, Epilady became an instant winner in the United States; 3.5 million units were sold the first year. The company looked unbeatable.

Then, hooked on its own success, EPI became manic. Over the next eighteen months, it introduced twenty-four major new products, including EpiPed (a foot massager), EpiSauna (a face steamer), and EpiSage (a shower massage). EPI introduced products what whitened teeth and those that remoistened dry skin. Sales rocketed to $200 million. Then, with no warning, and while articles in the media still heralded the company's extraordinary success, EPI Products filed for bankruptcy protection under Chapter 11.[1]

What went wrong? Epilady's instant success caused the company to believe itself invincible. It introduced too many products in too short a period. Analysis and planning went out the window, and there was no time to attend to details. None of the barrage of new products matched the success of the first; some cost the company large sums of money. Meanwhile, the problems that are an inevitable part of any big success cropped up; a legal fight over the licensing agreement, a lawsuit by a former partner, competition from low-cost copycat brands.[2] Even while fighting off these pressing problems, the company continued with its deluge of new products until it ran out of cash.

EPI is an almost classic case of manic behavior. The manic organization experiences abnormally expansive moods and levels of activity. It is on a self-induced and self-indulging high. The atmosphere reeks of grandiosity and excitement.

1. Cara Appelbaum, "EPI, a Victim of Its Success, Files Chapter 11," *Adweek's Marketing Week*, 10 September 1990, p. 28.
2. Dan Cook, "EPI Products: Fast Growth Leads to Growing Pains," *California Business*, February 1990, p. 15.

There is an acceleration in goal-directed activity that may make the future look very rosy. Even if based on very real success in the past, enthusiasm is visibly excessive. Little attention is given to the personal needs of the organization's members or to other important elements of work. Ethics and quality of work life may be ignored. Few stop to evaluate whether the organization can really do what it plans. Not infrequently, important details are overlooked. Decisions and operating processes become irrational and unaccountable. Mania can start with success, but it usually ends in failure.

The explosion of the *Challenger* is a particularly poignant example. When the shuttle program began, NASA's policy was that every launch had to be justified; that is, the burden was on those responsible to prove that a shuttle was safe to launch. Not surprisingly, the program had a 100 percent success rate.

Then, because there was never a failure, an unspoken assumption began to grow: "We cannot fail." By the time of the *Challenger* disaster, the original policy had turned around 180 degrees: The only way to stop a launch was to prove that it was *unsafe*. *Challenger* decision makers, frustrated by delays, decided to ignore small warnings. From the manic perspective, those warnings were minor details, not worth worrying about. Ironically, tragically, years of success led to failure.

The Starting Point for Mania: Success

Peter Drucker was one of the first management experts to declare that companies that continue to do what brought them success in the past would ultimately run into problems. Unfortunately, many organizations come to believe that past success makes success in the future inevitable. So they keep doing the same thing. For example:

* Many of the savings and loan failures of the 1980s were due to manic behavior. Organizations became hooked on actions that had produced success for them in the past. Past success produced feelings that they "just couldn't lose." This

overconfidence led to overlooking important details—and to massive failure.

* Adam Osborne started his computer company in 1978 and built it to $150 million in sales in less than a year. The product was a colossal success. A professional marketing association selected the company for an award as the outstanding marketer of the year. A vice-president at Osborne Computers said, "We're already into the next generation of computers. It's too late for any competitor to catch up." Six months later, the company went bankrupt doing essentially the same thing that had made it successful the previous year.

* Litton Industries had fifty-seven straight quarters of skyrocketing growth, reaching yearly sales of $1.8 billion by the mid-1960s. Suddenly, in 1968, everything came apart. Profits tumbled and Litton stock fell eighteen points in one week. What had gone awry? The astute noted that little had changed in Litton's structure or method of operating since it was a small company with annual sales of less than $1 million. Fumed CEO Charles B. "Tex" Thornton, "We do not want to change what we consider the right way to organize just because once in fifty-eight times something happened." Litton didn't change. The result? It wasn't until the mid-1970s that Litton got out of its slump, and then it was with an entirely new set of managers.[3]

* Robert Hall Clothes was the leading clothing discounter and the second largest apparel chain in the United States. By 1965, Robert Hall had 376 stores, and annual profits hit $14 million. In 1977, Senior Vice-President J. A. Bobbitt said, "We're going after the chains, Sears, Wards, and Penneys...."[4] But Robert Hall was manic. It disregarded changes in the business environment and in its customers. Its answer to change was continuing the same actions that had worked in the past, but now at an accelerating rate. Only a year after

3. Manfred F. R. Kets de Vries and Danny Miller, *Unstable at the Top* (New York: New American Library, 1987), pp. 2–5.

4. Robert F. Hartley, *Marketing Mistakes*, 2nd ed. (Columbus, Ohio: Grid, 1981), pp. 139–150.

Vice-President Bobbitt's pronouncement, the company filed for bankruptcy.

These examples illuminate one of the troubling aspects of manic behavior: While many observers, both inside and outside the company, can see what is happening, the organization itself may not recognize its mania until it is too late. On the contrary, the manic organization usually feels on top of the world. It shows inflated feelings of confidence, control, and ability. Only after it is cured—or goes bankrupt—does it realize just how serious the problem was.

Treating the Manic Organization

A manic organization is hard to treat. The organization is so convinced of future success that you cannot easily get it to accept reality. The obvious treatment—simply pointing out that the organization is manic—seldom works. First, people will give you reasonable-sounding explanations to justify every manic action that you question. If you persist in pointing out that the behavior is inappropriate, they will tell you that you just don't understand and that someone else will take full responsibility. Try to push your point even more and you will be told something like this: "If you're not going to help, then get out of the way." Finally, you will be shunted aside or fired. That doesn't help the organization, and it certainly doesn't help you. So the techniques for treating mania must be more subtle.

There are three alternatives for treating organizational mania:

1. Get a contract.
2. Get a plan.
3. Use anchoring techniques.

Gaining Control Through a Contract

Part of the problem in helping manic organizations is that it is so difficult to gain control. Manic organizations move very fast. Just as soon as you think you have gained a small measure of control in one area, the manic organization has already blundered into new areas. If this were true progress, control would be unnecessary. However, you are dealing with an overly excited organization that is paying little or no attention to the facts. Its only focus is on its own delusions of grandeur. So the situation may appear pretty hopeless. You are always behind.

To gain control over the mania, you must get the organization to commit to rules. One way to do this is by negotiating a contract. The first step is to refine your solution; then present it to the person in the company with the appropriate authority. Negotiate an agreement with that person, and use a contract to formalize that agreement. Your contract can be oral or written, but like all contracts it spells out what both parties have agreed to.

The secret is to present your idea in terms that support the company's perceived benefits. Your underlying goal is to impose some sort of control over an out-of-control organization, but you must package your idea so that it is acceptable to decision makers. The following stories about three different companies illustrate the process.

Joseph Sr. founded a small manufacturing company that was successful for many years when demand for its basic product was high. Then, when the product became something of a dinosaur and the company was sinking, Joseph Jr. took over from his father and saved the company by diverting it to another line of products. Over the next twenty years, sales of Joseph Jr.'s line leveled off; the market became saturated. Still, Joseph Jr. remained optimistic about the future of his products; in fact, he had grandiose plans for doubling his market.

Joseph III held a very junior position in the company but had a clear vision unimpeded by nostalgia. He could see that the company was headed downhill. He wanted to expand into other product lines, but he knew his father was dedicated to focusing on the product that had saved the company twenty years earlier. So he approached his father with a proposal: that he, Joseph III, be given the authority to explore new products.

His selling point was that this would help him overcome what his father perceived as his management inexperience.

So they struck a deal. Working with a small budget, Joseph III would develop one new product a year while still performing his other duties. This agreement was formalized with a contract memo spelling out the terms.

Joseph III got what he wanted—to gain control over a deteriorating situation—by giving the other party, in this case his father, something he wanted: experience for an inexperienced young man.

As it happens, Joseph Jr. died five years after this contract was finalized. Joseph III's five new product lines were by then moderately successful. Under the new leadership of its young president, the company increased sales tenfold in the next three years.

What if you're not the president's son? Can you still use this technique? Absolutely. Consider Louisa, a product manager in a consumer products company. Her supervisor, the research and development manager, insists on developing every new-product proposal that comes across his desk. This is classic mania at its worst. No organization has the time or resources to succeed with every possible new product.

Louisa knows that some of the proposed products will cost the company more than they are worth. She decides on her strategy: to develop a list of screening criteria through which all new ideas must pass. After some consideration, she settles on three criteria: sales potential of $50 million a year, a payback period of three years, and a return on investment of 20 percent. According to her idea, if proposals for new products don't meet these three criteria, they will be rejected.

But Louisa knows she can't go to her supervisor and say, in effect, "You're screwing up and I want to do things differently; here, sign this contract." Instead, she collects her facts, makes some sample cost projections, and presents her idea *as a proposal to increase profitability*. She's not hiding the facts: If the department focuses only on projects with greater sales potential, faster payback, and higher return on investment, it *will* increase profitability. So the R&D manager agrees to Louisa's proposal, and both sign off on a memorandum of agreement that details the specifics of the screening criteria.

What Louisa has done is to accomplish her goal—controlling the manic activity level of the department—by giving her manager something that is in his best interest to support. She focused her efforts on the part of the environment she could affect: her own department. But, by creating an island of rational behavior in a manic organization, this contract will ultimately have a positive impact on the entire company.

For one more example of the contract method, consider the case of Restaurant Developers Corporation (RDC). This Cleveland-based restaurant franchise became enamored with its own spiraling franchise sales in Cleveland in the mid-1980s. It soon began exhibiting manic behavior. Although a small company, RDC sunk millions of dollars into going national. Typically, it did inadequate research into the markets it was attempting to penetrate. It signed up anyone who could raise a buck, with little regard for other qualifications.

In California, RDC finally ran into the wall of reality. The menu was wrong for the California market, advertising costs were far higher than they had been in the Midwest, and sales were far lower. RDC franchisees failed left and right. Instead of pulling out, the company threw more cash at the problem. Sales effort soon outran the ability of the company to produce. The president was not concerned: "Don't worry about it," he said. "You guys sell 'em and we'll get 'em open."

The stock market crash in 1987 brought sales to a halt. RDC was on the ropes. At that point, the banks forced the company to turn the presidency over to its chief operating officer. He had his two feet firmly on the ground and hadn't bought into the manic thinking.

The new president's turnaround was based on the rules of treating manic behavior by using a contract. He called his contract a "standard of performance" (SOP). The SOP was a statement of quantified performance factors that were measured quarterly as well as once a year. Every member of the organization had an SOP, from the president right down to the secretaries. The SOPs weren't dictated; they were negotiated for mutual agreement. The results were worth the effort: The company became profitable again within one year, and revenue increased almost 31 percent in three years. *Success* magazine awarded the company the number one spot on its The Success Gold 100 in 1990.[5]

If you identify and confirm manic behavior, the sooner you can get a contract the better. A contract is a good containment device: It can act as an inoculation against the spread of manic behavior within your organization or department.

If you are in the lower ranks of the organization, draft a contract for your boss's approval. Emphasize the benefits from the company's perspective. Manic organization managers are all too ready to adopt any idea that meets their mania-driven view of where the organization should be headed.

If you are a manager, you can also initiate contract development for those who report to you. This saves you from appearing too arbitrary in killing off grandiose ideas, and it helps keep good undertakings within the bounds of reality. If the organization has already gone too far, rules agreement gained through a contract can save your company. The effect of the treatment is the same, no matter who initiates it.

Gaining Control Through a Plan

Just as a contract enables you to treat the mania through mutually agreed rules, a plan enables you to do the same with agreed methods. In essence, a plan provides a road map for your organization to follow, allowing it to reach its objective without making manic mistakes. A well-thought-through plan helps to rein in the mania, contain its disorganized behavior, and get the organization back on track. It makes the organization's action purposeful and directed toward attainable goals and objectives.

The content and overall format of the plan depend on the situation. If the problem being addressed is in a company's marketing function, what is needed is a marketing plan. If the production function is out of control, then you need an operations plan. If the entire company is floundering, maybe a strategic plan is the answer.

5. Richard Poe, "Grow Up or Die: How Disaster Made This Franchise Fight Back to Victory," *Success*, November 1990, p. 11.

The important point is to have a plan and use it. Without a plan in place to anchor its activities, any organization is vulnerable to spinning its wheels. A manic organization already is doing so; use the plan to set it on solid ground again.

If you are in authority, you may be tempted to have a planning organization put a plan together. Or you may think about having your entire organization work on the plan. That's the "total quality management" solution. In nonmanic situations, either of these solutions might work quite well. But a manic organization is going to come up with a manic plan, and a planning organization within a manic organization is probably manic too. If executed, a plan developed by people affected by manic thinking can result in more mania than you started with.

You, the change agent, must develop the draft of the plan yourself. Then you can invite input from others who may be affected by mania. You can do this whether you are a senior manager trying to treat the whole organization or a lower-level manager just trying to fix your own part of it. One caution: If you aren't in authority, don't mention *mania* or *manic organizations* in your plan. You want to control the manic behavior, not cause people to dig in and try to justify the craziness.

Your plan does not necessarily have to be complex—that depends on your situation—but it should address those important details that the manic organization ignores. The traditional elements of a plan include an executive summary, a table of contents, a situational analysis, objectives and goals, strategy and tactics for achieving the goals, and methods of implementing and controlling your suggestions. If you want to go all out, you can even include schedules and budgets.

If you are in authority, presenting your plan and getting commitment to it may not be much of a problem. If you aren't in authority, don't let that stop you. Put your plan together anyway. Present it in a low-key fashion to your boss, asking that it be sent up the chain to whatever level of the organization you are trying to treat. You may be amazed at the results. One of our graduate students had to drop out of the university because of lack of funds. Unfortunately, she ended up in a manic company. She put together a marketing plan that not only brought her company's mania under control but got her promoted to director of advertising in less than a year.

Gaining Control Through Anchoring Techniques

Sometimes you realize you could help a manic organization toward wellness if you could only get it to take certain actions. The only problem is that these actions run contrary to the organization's manic beliefs. Another method that can help you influence the company to take corrective actions is called anchoring.

An anchor is any kind of symbol that evokes a certain response, even though it may have little obvious connection to the response it stimulates. The bell that caused Pavlov's dog to salivate even when the dog was not in the presence of food was an anchor. Anchoring gave the bell a meaning that was the equivalent of smelling or seeing food.

Some anchors involve the presentation of a symbol at the height of an emotional experience. Afterward, this anchor will be linked to the emotion and can trigger it. An anchor can also be established without peak emotion if there is enough experience linking the symbol and what it comes to stand for. Anchors established this way are like the icons that represent different functions in some computer software. When you are first becoming familiar with the program, you must learn that one icon represents word processing, another represents graphics, another a file management process, and so on. After a while, your mind skips a step; it doesn't think "stands for." The icon equals the function just as the bell equals food for Pavlov's dog.

You probably experience the same phenomenon when you learn a foreign language. At first you learn that certain sounds in the foreign language stand for certain words in English. However, after a time your mind skips this intermediate step. You don't have to think of the English word or phrase first; instead, you think in that foreign language. The foreign words are now anchors that elicit thought responses.

One of the best-known anchors is the American flag. This

powerful symbol represents the United States; it stands for freedom, bravery, and the American way of life. Because a flag symbolizes something we feel strongly about, the presence of the physical flag can bring about a change in our emotional state. We may suddenly find a lump in our throat or tears in our eyes. That is why politicians who seek our vote surround themselves with the symbolism of the flag. They want the positive emotions the flag evokes to be identified with whatever agenda they are promoting.

Finding and Using Anchors

Through use of anchoring techniques, you can establish desired behavior patterns to eliminate manic behavior. In essence, you link the action you want the organization to take to the most powerful anchor you can find.

The first step is identifying the best anchor. It's not always a person. It may be a place, a concept, or a physical object. Any of these can symbolize something else that is emotionally identified with the organization.

Start by examining the essence of your organization. What does it really believe? What are its values? What does it stand for? Then, after you have precisely identified the basic meaning of your organization, you can look for anchors. What symbols represent that basic meaning?

You may find that it is represented by one or more of the following symbols:

- *A person*. The president, the CEO, the founder, or a leading personality in the organization.
- *A ceremony*. Annual sales dinners, award banquets, or retirement ceremonies.
- *A name*. Company jargon, nicknames.
- *An action*. Having the same motivational speaker every year at a meeting.
- *A physical symbol*. The company logo, the president's limo.
- *An attribute*. Smallness or largeness, past success, geographical location.

- *A way of doing business.* Emphasis on the family as part of the company.
- *A tradition.* A Christmas turkey, a company party.

Then, to treat the manic behavior, you must find a way of tying the anchor you have identified to the desired action. How you do this in actual practice depends on the situation you are facing. It's a matter of applying your ingenuity and common sense to the circumstances at hand. Let's look at just a few possibilities.

Suppose you're the sales manager for one division in your company. On paper, things look good—the annual sales numbers are high—but you sense that the underlying situation is shaky. The sales group has become so focused on bringing in new sales that it has grown manic, frantically pursuing new customers at the expense of servicing existing customers. Somehow you have to get the frenetic behavior under control.

Your company gives annual awards to the top sales representatives in each division, and they are highly prized. So there's your anchor: The awards are already established as something of value in the sales organization. To tie the anchor to action you want, you decide to create a new customer service award this year, with a special bonus for taking care of existing customers.

For another example, imagine that you're a project manager in an engineering company. Your department has long had a reputation for careful analysis of new projects; in fact, there's a vague feeling that this analysis is sometimes excessive and may be responsible for projects' taking too long to get under way. In unconscious reaction to this, the department has developed signs of manic behavior in the last year, rushing into action without sufficient planning. Critical details are being overlooked, creating all manner of production problems and budget overruns.

To bring the department back to sanity, you decide to reinvigorate the old reputation and make it a positive quality. You begin referring to your group as "The Analysts." In everything from the name on the front door to department memo pads, the new name is featured prominently. You even change the name of the department's softball team.

With this ever-present nickname serving as a reminder, gradually work habits begin to swing back. Soon others in the company begin to say things like "Maybe you should check with one of The Analysts." You have used the anchor of a particularly symbolic name to put a positive frame around the kind of behavior you want.

Another very powerful anchor in many organizations is a highly respected individual. If need be, you can use that person in your campaign to get the mania under control. That's exactly what happened at Honda a few years ago.

The Anchor at Honda

Nobuhiko Kawamoto took over the presidency of Honda in June of 1990. It was not the best of times. Demand for cars in Japan was slipping. The U.S. automobile market had been in a slump, and trade friction between the two countries was likely to affect future sales.

These challenging business conditions were especially troubling to the new president because he could see that the climate at Honda was manic (although he probably did not use that term). Honda had become one of the Big Three in the U.S. market after only twenty-one years. In Japan it had maintained its share while Toyota and Nissan had slowly slipped. Based on past success, the organization was beginning to think itself invincible.[6]

After analyzing the situation, Kawamoto concluded that the key for the future was rapid decision making. Up to then, the company had followed the consensus management techniques instituted by Honda's founder, thrashing problems out through all levels of management until agreement was reached. That style of management is extremely effective for gaining commitment. In the past, it was a major factor in the company's success. The trouble is that it takes a long time to make

6. Lindsay Brooke, "Tadashi Kume: 1990 Man of the Year," *Automotive Industries*, February 1990, pp. 58–64.

decisions this way. Also, as we mentioned earlier in this chapter, consensus decision making in a manic organization yields manic decisions.

President Kawamoto realized that past success did not guarantee success in the future. He concluded that the best way to forestall the approaching danger was to eliminate consensus management. It was a stunning move: a Japanese company converting to the American style of management just as many American companies were trying to copy Japanese techniques. He had to proceed carefully.

Kawamoto realized that a powerful anchor existed at Honda: its founder, Soichiro Honda. The company's employees trusted him with a reverence that went beyond simple respect. So, although he had the authority to proceed on his own, Kawamoto decided to enlist the help of this powerful anchor. He visited Honda in his Tokyo office and told him, "I'm sorry to say it, but not everything you said is correct now." He persuaded the founder to publicly agree to the changes he wanted. The 87,000 Honda employees reacted to their founder as expected: with respect and trust. They supported Kawamoto's changes although it meant a drastic break with past ways of doing business.[7]

Kawamoto's dramatic move did not instantly cure all problems; no treatment can do that. As we write, Honda's profits have fallen over the last year. But the company is doing better than everyone else in the automobile business. It gained more market share in the United States than any of its major competitors, and it gained share in Japan at the expense of Toyota, Nissan, and Mazda.

Summary

Manic organizations have an unrealistic sense that they cannot fail; often this is the result of success in the past. Overly excited, they rush ahead with grandiose plans and ignore

---

7. Alex Taylor III, "A U.S.-Style Shakeup at Honda," *Fortune*, 31 December 1991, pp. 115–121.

critical details. In their excessive enthusiasm, they are spinning out of control.

The primary treatment, then, is to gain control over the situation. Three techniques for doing that are:

1. Gaining commitment to rules through a contract
2. Gaining commitment to methods through a plan
3. Using anchoring techniques to link desired behavior to an established symbol

The key is to start early and control and contain the manic behavior as soon as possible.

3

On the Roller Coaster— Manic-Depression

Cycles are not, like tonsils, separable things that might be treated by themselves, but are, like the beat of its heart, at the essence of the organism that displays them.

—*Joseph A. Schumpeter, American economist*

Happiness, or misery, is in the mind. It is the mind that lives.
—*William Cobbett*, Grammar of the English Language

Being a part of a manic-depressive organization is a bit like being on the roller coaster at an amusement park: the thrill of climbing up, holding your breath because you know what's about to happen, the rush as you plunge down, the flat period at the bottom, then the thrill building as you start upward again.

However, a roller coaster is a game. It may not be everyone's idea of fun, but those who do like it are there by choice, and in any case they can get off when the ride is over. A business organization is not a game, and working for a company that suffers from manic-depression is not fun. It's more like a roller coaster ride that goes nonstop and ends by flying off the tracks at high speed, with tragic results.

Manic-depression is an illness in which the patient (individual or organization) is caught in a relentless cycle of mania, with its hyperactivity and unrealistic enthusiasms, and depression, with its abnormally low energy and feeling of apathy. The mania produces plans that are bound to fail because they are unrealistic, and that failure inevitably leads to depression.

It is normal to be enthusiastic about a project in which you have a lot of pride invested, and it is normal to feel depressed when that project fails. What is not normal is that in a manic-depressive organization the process repeats itself over and over.

Manic-Depression and the Discount Chain

In 1948, Eugene Ferkauf started a hole-in-the-wall luggage shop on the second floor of a nondescript building in East Manhattan. Seventeen years later, he headed a $700 million chain of discount department stores. Ferkauf called his company E. J. Korvette.

So impressive was Korvette's rise that at one time the Harvard Business School rated Ferkauf one of the six greatest American retail merchants. The School was to regret this enthusiastic assessment.

Eugene Ferkauf was a quiet, unassuming man, who built his company on the discount revolution that swept the country after World War II. He was an early proponent of management by wandering around. His informal, easygoing "foot patrol" gave on-the-spot guidance. And it would be hard to fault his personal leadership and ability to get the job done. His failure was a failure to diagnose and treat a severe case of manic-depression.

From 1962 to 1966, store space and sales volume at E. J. Korvette more than tripled. Ironically, it was during this period of the company's most dramatic growth that the symptoms of the disease first manifested themselves.

First came the mania. The company began to believe it could do anything. From so-called hard goods such as large and small household appliances, which the company well understood, it turned to goods about which it understood very little. Korvette plunged into fashion merchandise. Bedazzled by the potential for expansion and higher profit margins, the company paid little attention to detail in starting this new line. It did not note the increased need for management control that fashion and seasonal obsolescence would demand. Repeated markdowns and products that wouldn't sell eventually caused heavy losses. The company went into depression. It found its way out through another mania.

Before 1962, Korvette owned two supermarkets. In the manic phase of a new cycle, the company decided to locate supermarkets next to its discount stores, to profit further from its existing customers. Again Korvette acted with flair, adding twenty-two supermarkets almost overnight. And again, the pattern of manic behavior was inevitable. In its expansive mood, the company overlooked adequate analysis. E. J. Korvette opened its supermarkets without warehousing facilities. To avoid out-of-stock conditions, the supermarkets had to overstock. The basic rule of discounting, however, is to keep to a bare-bones-minimum, fast-moving inventory. Korvette stumbled again, losing $12 million in this operation in a single year. The company again fell into a depression.

There were more ups and downs. The company went into, and then got out of, discount furniture. It then tried unsuccessfully to copy Avon's success at selling cosmetics door-to-door.

In 1966, on one of the down cycles, E. J. Korvette merged with Spartan Industries. Two years later, Ferkauf was eased out. The new Korvette division of Spartan still had manic-depression, however. Convinced that its problems were due to an overappetite for expansion, it exhibited manic behavior in a new way. It decided that the key to greater profitability was to carry higher-priced lines. It abandoned its former merchandise and lost most of its former customers. The division lost almost $4 million and went into a new depression. At this point, Spartan finally sold Korvette's supermarkets.

Not long afterward, Spartan itself merged with a large real estate developer. The new owner changed the name of

the E. J. Korvette division by adding an *s* and dropping the
E. J. Try as you might, you can't hide from manic-depression by
changing your name. In successive years, the manic-depressive
behavior continued. The new "Korvettes" either lost money
or barely broke even every year. During the same period,
other discounters, like K mart, made a bundle.

Eventually, Korvettes was sold again, this time to Agache-
Willot, a French company. Agache-Willot didn't really cure
Korvettes' illness; it simply got rid of the illness by killing the
patient. It got out of the discount business and started over by
selling fashion-quality merchandise.[1]

Mania With Alternate Depression: A Major Challenge

As you might imagine, an organization that is alternately
manic and depressed is a major challenge, both to diagnose
and to treat. You will find traits of both mania and depression;
what you see depends on which part of the cycle you are
witnessing.

During the manic periods, the organization shows all the
symptoms of mania: overconfidence, fever-pitch enthusiasms,
grandiose plans coupled with unrealistic expectations and
little systematic planning. You never know what's going to
happen next. During the depressed periods that inevitably
follow, the organization lacks energy, negative thinking pre-
vails, and productivity and motivation take a nosedive. The
organization just sulks. Just when it is at its lowest, it shoots
off into space again.

Sometimes these companies can stay barely profitable
despite their disease. If so, they can go on that way for years.
This work/life roller coaster makes life terrifying for employees
as well as customers and suppliers. There is a resulting high
turnover all around.

Throughout the 1950s, A. C. Gilbert Company was one of

1. Robert F. Hartley, *Marketing Mistakes*, 2nd ed. (Columbus, Ohio: Grid,
1981), pp. 85–92; Lawrence A. Mayer, "How Confusion Caught Up With
Korvette," *Fortune*, February 1966, p. 154; "Korvettes Tries for a Little Chic,"
Businessweek, 12 May 1973, pp. 124–125.

the country's top ten toy makers. Founded in 1909, it was the proud producer of quality toys, including chemistry sets, American Flyer trains, and the world-famous Erector sets.

Then, in the early 1960s, something went wrong. In 1961 sales dropped from $12.6 million to $11.6 million, creating profits of only $20,011. The entire organization was depressed. Management knew it had to act, and it did—right into a manic mode. Gilbert introduced a phalanx of new toys, more than it had ever added in such a short period, and increased its sales force by 150 percent in less than a year. Everyone was excited about the new "wonder line" and felt certain that the troubles were over. They weren't: In 1962, sales dropped further, to $10.9 million, and losses increased to $281,000. Depression returned.

The next year, Gilbert introduced 50 new items, boosting the product line to an all-time 307-items high. Taking no chances, the company also spent $1 million to repackage its old product line. From the shop floor to the executive suite, Gilbert employees felt unstoppable. However, when the 1963 results came in, sales had declined even more, to $10.7 million, and losses increased to $5.7 million.

Now the company was really depressed. The board of directors hired Anson Isaacson as chief operating officer to turn the situation around. He had a terrific record as vice-president of Ideal Toy Company, which was larger than A. C. Gilbert. Isaacson dumped all the company salespeople and switched to manufacturing representatives to push the company's products. He also made major cuts in factory personnel. At the same time, he introduced twenty new products to a product line after pruning the old line extensively. The mood changed back to optimism. And in 1964, sales did increase, to $11.4 million. The company still had a loss, but it was lower: $1.9 million.

Boosted by this modest success, Gilbert moved fully into the manic side of the cycle. Isaacson increased the size of the product line again. He also spent $2 million for television advertising and $1 million on sixty-five thousand animated store displays. The high didn't last long. Sales for 1965 increased to $14.9 million, but losses increased too, to $2.9

million. For a company the size of Gilbert, that represents a massive loss.

To anyone who knows what to look for, these frantic stops and starts—high promotional expenditures and product introductions on the heels of losses and austerity measures—are clear signs of manic-depression. But, like many sick patients, Gilbert didn't recognize what was happening. And it was running out of money.

Convinced that he'd seen the light at the end of the tunnel, Isaacson bet the store on one big loan. By the terms of the loan, if the company didn't make a profit, the loan would be called and company assets sold to pay off the lenders. In 1966, losses were almost $13 million. The once proud company went under. Today's families can still buy Erector sets, but they buy them from CBS, Inc., not A. C. Gilbert.[2]

Treating the Manic-Depressive Organization

You can't help an organization suffering from manic-depression with the techniques used to treat either mania or depression alone. If you try, you'll only succeed in driving the organization into a higher mania or a deeper depression.

To treat the manic-depressive organization, you must dampen the swing between the two extremes. In general terms, you do this by assuming control: applying structure, discipline, and strict controls. At the same time, you should use motivational routines to maintain morale. As a practical matter, this is easier to do if you hold a position of authority in the organization. Three specific techniques are recommended:

1. *Exercise strict discipline but give quick recognition for the type of action you want.* This is the old "carrot and stick" approach. By maintaining strict control through reward and punishment, you can regulate the degree of excitement or depression until normalcy returns.

2 Robert F. Hartley, *Marketing Mistakes, 2nd ed.* (Columbus, Ohio: Grid Publishing, 1981), pp. 181–190; "Toymaker A. C. Gilbert Co. Poor Loser?" *Sales Management,* 1 May 1966, pp. 27–28.

2. *Focus on your organization's real purpose rather than on short-term profits.* Years ago Harvard's Theodore Leavitt proposed that the purpose of a business was to create a customer. Profit is necessary to do this, but profit should not be the ultimate goal of the business.[3] If you focus on serving the customer, then growth, sales, and profits will follow almost automatically. In any case, such a focus is incompatible with grandiosity.

3. *Use directive leadership.* Participatory management, highly effective in healthy organizations, does not work with the manic-depressive organization. Until the organization is well, you must be a take-charge, "Theory X" style manager.

How to Use the Back-to-School Treatment

A specific strategy that works in many manic-depressive situations is what we might call the back-to-school treatment. The idea is simple: Back-to-basics training not only helps employees do their jobs better but also reestablishes discipline and creates a new framework for control. The training forces the "students" to focus on the company's real purpose. Also, because organizational members who participate in the training usually enjoy increased success on the job, there is a direct, positive effect on morale.

Military organizations have long used the back-to-school concept successfully. Recently the Air National Guard lost several F-16 aircraft for a variety of reasons. When this happens, the standard procedure is to send the organization back to school. In this case, the commander of the Air National Guard immediately stopped normal training. He ordered a return to basic F-16 flying before resuming the regular mission training schedule. If you saw the movie *Twelve O'Clock High,* you saw a fictional illustration of the same concept. Gregory Peck took command of a B-17 group that had taken heavy losses in combat over Germany. His first action was to get the

3. Theodore Leavitt, *The Marketing Imagination* (New York: Free Press, 1983), p. 6.

unit relieved from combat duty. He then put his whole organization through a basic combat flying training program.

Civilian organizations have used the same strategy to control and dampen manic-depressive cycles. An academic department at a university was battered by personnel and budgetary change. In seeking funding, the department alternately pursued first-rate research and quality teaching. These incompatible goals drove it back and forth between mania and depression, ensuring that the department would perform neither function well. A new chairperson cured the organization by first getting it to take basic training in both teaching and research and then focusing on one goal.

A division manager "fixed" the manic-depression in his automobile assembly plant. He set up basic training on customer orientation and required all employees to attend. They learned to look beyond quick fixes; they forgot the depression of past failures. Instead, they concentrated on their real mission.

What Middle Managers Can Do

Remember, the essential element in treating manic-depressive organizations is to dampen and then to gain control of the mood swings. The techniques for accomplishing this—discipline, structure, directive leadership—are basically the province of senior executives. What if you see a problem but are not in top management? Then you need to break the manic-depressive state of decision makers who have the authority to correct the problem. Somehow, you must get them to pay attention to reality, and you must do it without criticizing. Even the most fair-minded executive is likely to get defensive if you point out that she is exhibiting manic-depressive behavior. You are likely to get ignored—or fired. Clearly, the task is difficult, but if you can pull it off, you can help both your company and your own reputation. Here's the story of one middle manager who succeeded.

A certain small company made personal equipment for the military. Its past success was based on winning government research and development contracts for product development. The company would then use the knowledge and expertise it gained during the development to be more efficient in production. On future bids for production runs, it could build the item more cheaply than its competitors could. So far, so good.

Unfortunately the company had a string of failures in new-product development. These soon became part of the classical mood swings of the manic-depressive. The company would identify a potential contract on which to bid and would immediately go into a period of high excitement and activity. Other developmental work was delayed or abandoned, and maximum effort went to the new target. Overtime became the normal way of operating. Depression inevitably followed when the company either failed to win the contract or won it but realized that the work would be far more difficult than expected. In its depressed state, the company would make serious mistakes in development. Previous work neglected during the manic cycle would come due, deepening the depression. This would last until a new target contract was identified, and the cycle would repeat itself.

Top managers didn't recognize the sickness. They blamed all the problems on bad luck. "We're doing everything anybody could expect," one commented. "Research and development is always difficult."

A middle manager in this company succeeded in putting things right. He mandated a new procedure for his department: full product development schedules for potential new products as they were identified. With these schedules, staff members were able, for the first time, to compare costs, future sales, and likelihood of success for all new projects; they could also evaluate the new projects against ongoing work.

This rigorous analysis brought several beneficial effects. First, with knowledge of what full development of ongoing projects was actually costing in financial and human resources, the department understood the reasons for its own past failures. It prioritized ongoing work and concentrated on high-value new projects that could be completed within needed time frames. As performance improved, morale soared.

But the benefits extended beyond this one department. It often happens in troubled companies that one healthy area stands head and shoulders above the rest, its superior performance all the more noticeable because it is so markedly different. Little by little, other departments began to adopt the control procedures, and eventually even the top managers realized the consequences of their past actions. The mood swings lessened in amplitude and eventually stopped.

Eight months later, the company bid a major contract with a government agency that had vowed never to use the company again. Not only did the company win the contract, but it was fully prepared to accomplish it. The company's newfound sanity resulted in one of its most successful products.

Summary

If you want to treat a manic-depressive organization, you have your work cut out for you. The idea is to get control and dampen the swing between the two polarities. Structure, discipline, and controls are your watchwords. But you must maintain morale and the organization's self-image at the same time. This makes treatment tricky.

Treatment techniques should be based on the following:

1. Strict discipline
2. Focus on the organization's real purpose for existence
3. Use of directive rather than participative leadership tactics

The back-to-school concept provides a framework for many of these treatment approaches.

It is especially difficult to treat a manic-depressive organization when you are not its boss. You must use determination, ingenuity, and, most of all, subtlety in helping those in authority to recognize reality.

4

Confusion and Chaos— Schizophrenia

Schizophrenia cannot be understood without understanding despair.

—R. D. Laing, The Divided Self

Did you know that *bedlam*, a word we now use as a synonym for *chaos*, was originally the name of a hospital for the insane in eighteenth-century London? Bedlam is a fair description of a schizophrenic company. Its conduct is disorganized and chaotic. Nothing seems to make sense. Everywhere you turn, you see illogical, unpredictable behavior. Working for a schizophrenic company can be very stressful, especially if you take your job and your future seriously.

Sometimes a schizophrenic company displays some symptoms similar to the manic organization. However, it is easy to distinguish between the two. The manic may not have much of a hold on reality, but at least it thinks it knows where it is headed. The schizophrenic company doesn't have a clue; worse, it doesn't seem to care. To state that in business terms, the manic organization is driven by a mission that is wildly unrealistic, but at least it has one. Schizophrenic organizations *have* no mission, or if they do, it is wholly incoherent.

Penn Square Bank began as a small operation in a shopping mall in Oklahoma City. The energy crisis and deregulation of oil and gas drilling during the presidency of Jimmy Carter fueled its rise. It grew by lending money to small, independent oil and gas companies who couldn't otherwise get financing for exploration and drilling.

As it grew, Penn Square became schizophrenic. The CEO, William P. "Beep" Jennings, began selling loans to larger banks as fast as he received them. He appointed as gas and oil loan officer a man named William G. Patterson, known as Monkey Brains. It is said that Patterson was "real fun" to do business with. Like the animal from which he received his nickname, he sometimes threw food. On one occasion he sat on his heels in his office and began howling in front of potential borrowers. "If you're going to treat us like dogs," he explained, "we're going to act like dogs." He sent a "visitors committee" to the airport to greet out-of-town customers. As they came off the plane, these visitors were met by a group of young, provocatively dressed women asking, "Want to have some fun?"

Patterson's approach to his job was unusual, to say the least. Not only did he loan money without collateral, he sometimes gave borrowers more money than they asked for. After a while, Patterson even stopped worrying about loan applications, which he considered an unnecessary formality. One borrower was given a loan even though the interest payments were five times greater than his income. Another borrower, overdrawn more than $1 million on his account, quit making interest payments altogether. Still, the bank didn't seem to worry; its borrowers had "character," and these were "character" loans.

It isn't clear whether Jennings knew exactly what was going on, but bank auditors began to worry. Audits found insufficient capital, ongoing problem loans, and other abnormalities. "Beep" Jennings promised to get things shaped up. Meanwhile, loan volume reached $3 billion and was growing. Jennings passed all the loans on to larger banks. When bank expenses exceeded bank income, he sold bank stock to keep going.

Suddenly, on July 5, 1982, it was all over. Penn Square Bank closed and was liquidated. Company officers were indicted, and stockholders lost everything. Uninsured depositors got a few cents on the dollar. The huge amount of loans that Penn Square had passed on to other banks caused reverberations through the banking industry.

The Schizophrenic Organization

The popular image of schizophrenia as "split personality," while colorful, is inaccurate; a person whose personality is "split" into two or more parts actually suffers from a different illness. So don't go looking for a schizophrenic organization to show several different personalities. What you will find, always, is an organization that lacks the right structure to get things done. Success, if it occurs, happens randomly and by chance. It is always temporary.

If you are ever in an organization that has become schizophrenic, you'll never forget it. *Chaos* is the operative word. One department may not be aware of what the other is doing. Worse, it may not even care. If the organization once had clear goals and objectives, there's little sign of them now. There may be quite a bit of hyperactivity, but it leads nowhere.

One manager described his schizophrenic company well: "Our company is like a galley ship without a drummer. We've got some people rowing at full blast, some at one-half beat, some at one-quarter beat, and some dead beats. Also, the captain is steering by the wake."[1]

Schizophrenic organizations chew people up. The stress level is horrendous. On a day-to-day basis, people rarely know what to expect. Everyone is at risk for demotion, firing, a nervous breakdown, early retirement, or worse. As with Penn Square Bank, the illness can get so far out of hand that the inevitable blowup makes waves outside the confines of the organization. Remember, executives and other employees at Penn Square Bank topped off their experience with a schizophrenic company by being indicted.

1. Peter Hay, *The Book of Business Anecdotes* (New York: Facts on File, 1988), p. 143.

Most organization members recognize these dangers and feel their lack of security very strongly. Many leave as soon as they perceive a way out. Not even outsiders like to associate with schizophrenic companies. They are concerned that when the situation finally blows, it will take them with it. So suppliers and customers frequently remain affiliated only as long as they must.

Several years ago, a well-known publishing house displayed unmistakable signs of schizophrenia. For example:

• Communication between departments was abysmal; many things fell through the crack. One author got a glowing recommendation for his new book from a celebrity, along with permission to use the recommendation. Some months after the book was published, with the endorsement featured prominently on the dustcover, the author received a call from the marketing manager. She had just seen this "wonderful endorsement" and wanted to use it to promote the book. Had the author obtained permission from the celebrity? He pointed out that not only had he received permission but the testimonial was already in boldface type on the dustcover.

• There was little coordination among editors, and it wasn't clear who was in charge. The editors often contracted with authors for books that competed with each other, and the company published such books at the same time. New books were published that competed with old ones still selling well. The net gain in sales? Almost zero.

• As profits declined, the parent organization sought to sell off its publishing division. This was no secret, so management wisely decided to keep employees informed. However, the information given was both inaccurate and conflicting. Morale drooped along with sales and profits. Employees, expecting they would eventually be fired anyway, left in droves. At last, only one editor remained. He was told he had been retained only because his salary was the lowest. He left on his own as soon as he could. The marketing manager was told she would be let go as soon as a buyer for the publishing division could be found. When she left on her own with the last editor, no one was available to do either job. Not surprisingly, no buyer ever appeared.

Treating the Schizophrenic Organization

If you remember that schizophrenia and mania show rather similar symptoms, you probably won't be surprised to learn that the fundamental treatment for both disorders is also similar: In both cases you must firmly regain control.

The treatments for gaining control over schizophrenic organizations require that you go back to the beginning: Reaffirm your organization's mission, and make sure that your best energy is focused on actions that support the mission and its objectives. That seems simple enough, but it's a big order, so in this chapter we break it into steps. We also find that frequently treatment involves some form of restructuring. The treatments, then, are as follows:

1. Gain control over mission.
2. Set objectives.
3. Support the mission.
4. Focus on the center of gravity.
5. Restructure the organization.

Let's look at each of these approaches in turn.

Gaining Control Over Mission

To treat a schizophrenic organization, you must begin by getting a firm grip on your mission. Noted management consultant Peter Drucker recommends that you begin any organizational analysis by asking a single question: "What business are we in?" Even if you are not running the company, your unit has a mission, and it must somehow support the company's mission. Ask yourself, "What are we really trying to do here?" The answers to this question help you identify your mission.

Donald W. Brinckman bought a schizophrenic little company that sold a device for degreasing parts to service stations. The company was losing $75,000 a year. It had no mission, other than selling the product, and no specific objectives. The company had lots of activity and many ideas, but it was going nowhere.

He probably wouldn't have bought the company if he hadn't spotted its fantastic distribution network and the potential to grow this network further. He offered the owners $25,000, and they jumped at it. Then the new owner began treatment. First he decided what business he was really in: "We changed our mission to become the world's biggest processor of hazardous waste fluids. In 1987, revenue hit $333 million, and we bought the biggest oil re-refining plant in North America."[2]

Setting Objectives

Once you define a mission that you know makes sense, you can proceed with setting objectives to support that mission. Each objective is a short-term minimission. Objectives define precisely what you are aiming to accomplish, and when.

Maybe your organization is the loan department of a bank. One of your objectives might be to develop a database that includes size and number of loans, borrowers, risk factors, and key dates. If Penn Square Bank had taken this one simple step, it might have avoided a major calamity.

Maybe you are a principal in a small architectural company. Your organization's mission is to design affordable and environmentally appropriate housing for homeowners in your region. Some objectives might be:

- Add a landscape architect to your staff.
- Set up a satellite office in the neighboring county.
- Conduct a survey of homeowners to find out what features they find especially appealing.
- Develop ongoing relationships with local policymakers who are involved in housing and land use issues.

2. "On the Path to Opportunity," *Success*, June 1992, p. 16.

Or perhaps you are the assistant director of a neighborhood mental health clinic. Your mission is to improve the mental and emotional health of individuals and families in your service area. To get a handle on this broad goal, you might come up with objectives like these:

- Prepare a demographic survey of the service area to develop accurate data on income levels and family size.
- Recruit graduate students in psychology to serve as volunteer counselors.
- Evaluate current clinic space in light of projected needs and future programs.
- Coordinate your agency's children's programs with the counseling and mental health services now in place in the school system.

Frequently, you will come up with more objectives than you have the time and resources to accomplish. To narrow them down, list the benefits you will gain if you achieve each objective and the costs you will experience if you don't. Using these lists, decide which objectives offer the most benefits and the least cost. Then pick several that you can reasonably accomplish.

Supporting the Mission

The disorganization that exists in schizophrenic organizations leads to many strange effects. Perhaps one of the strangest is employees' engaging in activities that have little to do with the success of the corporate mission. A subordinate organization, a project, or a program may consume considerable resources while having nothing to do with the mission or even while working against it.

We have seen an organization whose mission was research and development engaged in all-out production activities, and vice versa. We have seen companies whose mission was marketing armored cars frantically engaged in the production of Jacuzzis. We once saw a management consultant happily diffusing his efforts by trying to sell his clients soap.

Small companies aren't the only ones exhibiting this brand of schizophrenia. McDonnell-Douglas, one of the United States's leading developers of custom spacecraft for the government, once went all out to develop and produce a high-volume nonspace product, with predictable results: multimillion-dollar losses.

When you take the time to get really clear on your mission and set specific objectives, you're much more likely to notice actions that are at odds with the big picture. And that is the crux of this particular treatment: Make sure that all actions really support the mission.

David Rotenberg, a Langhorne, Pennsylvania, jeweler, opened a new store in an upscale neighborhood. He set his sights on offering distinctive merchandise in an elegant atmosphere to affluent customers. To achieve this, he hired a noted architect to create an elegant store with expensive fixtures. But then he ran newspaper ads that emphasized low discounted prices. When customers became confused and sales started to stall, he quickly realized his error: The advertising was not supporting the overall mission. He changed his tactics and got the mission back on track.

Looking back over his experience later, Rotenberg offered this advice: "Decide what you want to be, then be it."[3] That's a good way of summarizing this treatment. Remember, there's a lot you can't control, and you shouldn't waste your time trying. However, make certain that whatever you personally can control supports your mission and objectives. If it doesn't, change it at once.

Focusing on the Center of Gravity

In schizophrenic organizations, chaos is everywhere. Managers often feel overwhelmed; they juggle too many corporate balls and are in danger of losing everything. The solution is focus: Choose the really important objectives and concentrate your energies on them. Realize that you cannot be successful

3. Hedda T. Schupak, "Marketing Clinic: Avoid 'Schizophrenic' Marketing," *Jewelers Circular Keystone* December 1990, p. 71.

in every single effort that is going on around you. Recognize that some pieces are simply outside your control. Stop trying to control the uncontrollable. If a project threatens to become impossible, get rid of it.

A corporate recruiter we know returns year after year to interview potential job candidates at a prestigious university. Over the years, this recruiter has interviewed several hundred students from this school, but his company hasn't hired a single one; it can't afford the going salary rate. This recruiter is on an impossible mission. He can't control the salary offers, so he'd be much better off to simply stop recruiting at this university.

Instead of wasting time in areas you can't control, you should be focusing on critical efforts. We call these critical efforts the center of gravity (COG), borrowing a concept from Karl von Clausewitz, the nineteenth-century military strategist. In analyzing the events of the Napoleonic Wars, Clausewitz found that in every battle situation there was a center of gravity, the one critical juncture to which ultimate success or failure could be traced. Victory at the COG would ensure victory everywhere, and so Clausewitz recommended concentrating resources at the COG. If you stop trying to control what you can't, or shouldn't, you have more resources to concentrate at the COG.

Once-mighty Mattel had a numbing $391 million loss in 1983 as the video game business went into a nosedive and its Intellivision investment collapsed. Mattel went over the edge. According to one analyst, the company began dumping new products on its retailers without proper testing. Then it quit reacting to feedback in the market. Competitors noted that they weren't listening very well and were slow to respond. The losses continued: $8.3 million in 1986, $113 million in 1987. Retailers lost confidence in the company; some predicted its imminent demise.[4]

Enter John Ameran to Mattel's helm. In his first year, he laid off 22 percent of his work force, pruned management,

4. Joe Mandese, "Playing Favorites," *Marketing and Media Decisions*, March 1990, pp. 75–79.

and shut down more than half of Mattel's production facilities around the world. He cut the number of products offered in half and concentrated his efforts on the COG. He said that it was the smartest thing they did. Sales of Hot Wheels increased by $40 million; that's 75 percent over the preceding year. Similarly, Barbie doll sales were up by $45 million, a 30 percent increase. Profits soared. *California Business* said Ameran had pulled off "the most dramatic turnaround in the history of the toy business."[5]

The center of gravity may be a core product line, as with Mattel. It may also be a critical area of weakness that can cripple the organization if not improved. Look at the experience of a relatively small manufacturing company.

The Rogers Corporation, founded in Connecticut, makes highly innovative electronic and automotive components. Some years ago, in an effort to reduce labor costs, it moved its manufacturing operations into Mexico. Unfortunately, the Mexican operation soon became schizophrenic. Scrap rate was running at 25 percent of yield, and on-time delivery hovered between 35 and 40 percent.

Daniel Murillo was acting operations manager at one Rogers Corporation plant in Mexico during this period. He recalled, "Although the supervisors were responsible for the training of their people, because quality and on-time delivery were so low, they didn't have time to devote to training—so quality and delivery suffered. It was a vicious circle." The stress on employees was terrific, causing an astronomical turnover rate of 20 percent and further contributing to inferior quality.

Rogers "cured" this illness by focusing on the center of gravity. Rather than trying to control everything that was out of control all at once, it concentrated on a few critical objectives, such as training. In three short years, the situation was completely turned around. Today, quality is very high. In fact, the company quit measuring scrap as a percentage of yield

5. Robert Lindstrom, "Toy Town Turnaround," *California Business*, December 1989, pp. 30–40.

and now does it by defective parts per million. On-time delivery is approaching 96 percent. Productivity increased by 67 percent. Turnover is less than half what it was and is still declining.[6]

Restructuring the Organization

You almost always need to restructure when the organization is schizophrenic. This is true because the old structure is usually part of the problem.

Zebra Technologies makes bar code label printers and their accessories for the automatic identification market. Products are engineered in the United States, but most of the manufacturing was in Japan. Originally, this structure made sense. But then the Japanese operation began showing signs of schizophrenia. Lines of authority were crossed; communication was confused and disorganized. These problems manifested themselves in quality problems in the Japanese-made products.

Zebra's solution was to restructure, by relocating its manufacturing operations to the United States. Five years later, Senior Vice-President Gerhard Cless was able to report close to 100% defect-free machines in the U.S. In 1991, Zebra's total warranty cost was less than $50,000 on sales of $45.6 million, all due directly to restructuring. Explained Stewart A. Shiman, vice president of operations, "When our products were mostly made in Japan, it was hard to communicate halfway around the world and get problems corrected."

Zebra acted with a leveraged treatment. With this one restructuring action, the company lowered the cost of manufacturing, achieved higher quality, and gained more flexibility to respond to its customers.[7]

---

6. William H. Miller, "Textbook Turnaround," *Industry Week*, 20 April 1992, pp. 11–12.

7. Brian S. Moskal, "The Return of a Native," *Industry Week*, 6 July 1992, pp. 11–12.

Summary

The basis of schizophrenia is disorganization or misorganization; it shows up most commonly as confusing, exhausting chaos. Treating this ailment involves gaining control of the organization and where it is headed through these approaches:

1. Gain control over the mission.
2. Set objectives.
3. Ensure that all actions support the mission.
4. Stop efforts to control what you can't control; instead, focus on the center of gravity.
5. Restructure the organization.

5

"They're Out to Get Us!"—Paranoia

Suspicion generates dark devils.
—Japanese proverb

Paranoids not only have enemies, they create them.
—William A. Cohen

An organization that routinely treats everyone with suspicion and assumption of malicious intent is paranoid. Few in the organization or outside it are trusted. There is a feeling that people are out to get something they shouldn't or that they want to do harm to the organization. Among employees, fear becomes pervasive. The environment turns hostile. For its part, the organization puts more emphasis on protecting what it has than on performance, reasonable risk taking, and accomplishment. In a competitive business climate, this can lead to disaster.

Benson Engineering did highway construction worldwide. Over time, it developed extensive contacts with influential people abroad, which significantly increased the business that the company got through referrals. Then a senior manager resigned and started a competitive company. Some of his new work came through Benson's referral network. Almost overnight, Benson became paranoid. It limited all contacts with foreign personnel except by top management. Managers working abroad were discouraged from any contact with local nationals except when absolutely required. Even then, they had to obtain prior approval from top management back in the United States. They couldn't even accept an invitation to a cocktail party without wiring the home office for approval. Weekly, managers had to forward logs of all contacts, with minute details of what went on. Failure to do so was grounds for dismissal.

In one sense, this paranoid behavior was successful: It did prevent further loss of business to the former employee's company. However, Benson's own staff was thoroughly demoralized by the company's behavior, and their performance showed it. Costs exploded. Time slippages and performance shortfalls became almost routine. Project profitability declined. Ironically, new business from referrals dwindled and then disappeared altogether. Finally a competitor bought the ailing company. By then, it was barely functioning.

A look at a paranoid organization will uncover:

- Suspicion
- Lack of trust
- Significant fear of outside intentions
- Security as a primary concern

Paranoia at GM

For many years, General Motors was the largest company in the world. It consistently outperformed its U.S. rivals in almost every measurement. Most years, it captured over 50 percent of the automotive market, twice Ford's share and four times Chrysler's. It became the prototype for cartoonist Al Capp's spoof company owned by General Bullmoose. When Capp had General Bullmoose say, "What's good for General Bullmoose is good for the U.S.A.," everyone knew what company he was satirizing.

Then, in the 1960s, something began to go wrong. GM's legendary chairperson, Alfred E. Sloan, had built the business on the cornerstone of centralized strategy but decentralized control. Sloan's successors turned that policy upside down. Corporate leaders stopped providing strategic vision and instead began centralized monitoring and control of the GM divisions.

What was behind this policy shift? Paranoia. At that time Americans' fascination with smaller, foreign-made cars was becoming apparent, and the leaders of the various GM divisions wanted to develop their own small models to keep up with consumer demands. The corporate leaders had other ideas on how to meet this challenge, and the divisional managers' proposals were viewed as revolt.

In this uneasy climate, full-blown paranoia began to grow. Corporate officers became convinced that the division managers wanted to dismantle the company; their solution was to tighten central controls even more. The more the managers fought, the more determined the paranoid company was to maintain control.

The disease spread throughout the organization, producing excessive rivalry among divisions. Suspicion and rivalry also developed among functional specialties, with finance and accounting conspiring against engineering and marketing and vice versa. It wasn't long before the effects of all this showed up in the product. Between 1978 and 1982, GM recalled 70 percent of its cars. During the same period, Chrysler and Ford recalled less than 50 percent.[1]

The Insidious Nature of Paranoia

An organization can continue for a long time with a kind of low-grade paranoia. It may manage to avoid a major crisis, but it probably falls far short of its potential. Even if mildly profitable, it is distinguished by its long-term lackluster performance. Meanwhile, the abnormal behavior may come to be thought of as normal. A true paranoid organization sincerely

1. Charles G. Burck, "Will Success Spoil General Motors?" *Fortune*, 22 August 1983, p. 98.

believes that its bizarre behavior is normal and necessary. Members seeking to create change will probably find that their judgment is questioned: what is worse, they may actually become suspect themselves.

The paranoia in an organization can progress to a point where everyone is suspected of having an ulterior motive. Information of almost any type is a secret, not to be trusted to anyone. This plainly works against cooperation and involvement. It prohibits the sharing of information that enables employees to strive toward a common organizational goal. It discourages employees from working on mutually rewarding projects. It can trigger catastrophe: Employees do what they are told to do even if they know the results will be disastrous.

Ironically, this "top secret" atmosphere can actually *cause* serious security leaks. Members of the organization, encouraged to be careful of everything, soon are unable to tell the difference between harmless information and real corporate secrets. When all information is devalued to the same low denominator, slips are inevitable.

The effects of paranoia on organizational profitability are horrendous. Innovation is actively discouraged. Productivity sinks under the weight of unnecessary security procedures. In the stifling atmosphere of distrust and unwarranted suspicion, the best employees leave in disgust, or they try to sponsor change and get fired for their trouble.

Here are just a few real-life examples.

* Robert Oppenheimer, director of the program that produced the atomic bomb during World War II, lost his security clearance. No reason was ever given. For years, he was deprived of government work; perhaps more important, the United States was deprived of his services.

* A talented engineer was fired because he revealed his salary to another employee. His company, like many paranoid organizations, had an unreasonable fear of employee collusion. The engineer was promptly hired by a competitor, and the products he proceeded to design eventually helped his new company take massive sales away from the company that fired him.

* A high-tech company kept full knowledge and description of forthcoming products so secret that two divisions spent thousands of dollars developing essentially identical products.

Paranoid behavior may be more prevalent than we think. Kathleen Ryan and Daniel Oestreich surveyed employees in twenty-two organizations around the United States. Seventy percent of them said that they "bit their tongues" at work because they feared the repercussions of speaking out. Says Ryan, "If you want people to do only what they're told, fear may not be a bad motivator. But if the success of your business depends on people doing far more than what they're told, that's not good."[2]

Lessons Learned From a Game

In our seminars, we sometimes have students participate in a management game designed to reveal just how destructive paranoia can be, except that we don't tell them the real purpose until the end.

We start by giving teams of participants five minutes to view a complex structure built of children's blocks. We then give each team a sack of blocks and tell the teams to replicate the structure from memory. The team that does this in the shortest time wins.

We give all participants a sealed envelope containing a slip of paper, and we instruct them to look at the slip and return it to one of us without comment. We tell them that, for each team, one slip of paper is marked with an X. The team member who receives that slip of paper is designated the spy. No one else knows who the spy is.

The spy's duties are to impede the building of the structure by inciting confusion, giving erroneous input, being clumsy, and using any other means he can think of without

2. Therese R. Welter, "They're Afraid of You and Their Work Suffers Because of It,'" *Industry Week*, 1 October 1990, p. 11.

being so obvious as to get caught. If accused, the spy can deny being a spy or say nothing, as he wishes. Only if all other team members unanimously agree to the identity of the spy can they drop him from their team.

Teams almost always catch their spies and throw them off their teams. After the competition, we tell them the truth: There were no X's on any of the slips of paper. All of the "spies" caught and dropped were innocent. Not only did the paranoia engender suspicion and fear, but it resulted in the loss of a potentially productive team member.

Treating the Paranoid Organization

To treat paranoia, you must get the organization to reject its illness, both emotionally and intellectually. We have found the following treatments effective:

1. Build trust.
2. Use the rule of reciprocity.
3. Employ reality confrontation.
4. Redirect.

Building Trust

Since the key symptom of organizational paranoia is suspicion and distrust, the primary treatment is to build a sense of trust among members of the organization. Basically, the way to do this is to get them away from the organization so they can begin to relate to one another in different and healthier ways.

If you are in a position of authority, you can devise activities that involve the entire organization, such as a companywide picnic or a softball or bowling league. If you are at a lower level, you probably will work more with individuals. The process still works: One by one, get people away from the company so that they can see you in a different environment. Over a period of time, go out to lunch with different people. Don't have an agenda for these lunches. The idea is to build trust by simply getting to know one another. Getting together socially with employee families is another method. Again, don't try to sell any ideas you have during these outings. Just get to know the other person and let him or her get to know you.

Using the Rule of Reciprocity

Professor Robert B. Cialdini at Arizona State University coined the term *rule of reciprocity* for an unusual phenomenon: Human beings in our society must reciprocate anything done for them or they feel discomfited. If you've ever seen members of the Hare Krishna sect giving out flowers at airports, you've seen this rule in action. A Hare Krishna walks up and pins a flower on an unsuspecting donor-to-be. If the person tries to return the flower, the Hare Krishna says, "It's our gift, but if you want to help, you can give us a donation." This simple tactic works far more often than it fails.[3]

You can use the rule of reciprocity to treat organizational paranoia. Here's how one very smart manager did it.

In 1975, a team of entrepreneurs founded Supercuts, Inc. The idea was revolutionary: Replace the traditional barbershop and beauty shop with unisex hairstyling salons featuring low prices and walk-in, no-appointment convenience. Quality and high standards were the hallmarks. New Supercuts franchisees had to attend a five-day training course even if they were already licensed. Supercuts was on to something, and sales and profits took off.

Unfortunately, as Supercuts expanded, it began to show a leaning toward paranoia. It particularly suspected its own franchisees, fearing that every suggestion had the ulterior motive of increasing franchisee profitability at the expense of the corporation. Convinced that the corporation would forever ignore their ideas, the store owners formed an association to represent their interests. The corporation didn't like that very much either. Soon the whole corporation was paranoid, top to bottom. More disagreements led to a class action lawsuit by the franchisees.

By 1987, Supercuts was in deep trouble. Sales had dropped. Morale was low. Productivity was down. The atmosphere was

---

3. Robert B. Cialdini, *Influence* (New York: Quill, 1984), pp. 42–43.

hostile. Some franchise owners thought the company wouldn't survive its illness.

Enter a treatment specialist by the name of Betsy Burton. She had held a succession of top management jobs in the beauty industry since getting her MBA at the University of Chicago. Knights-Bridge Partners, Inc., a Chicago-based investment company, bought the ailing corporation and brought Burton in as CEO.

Burton met with the franchisees even before the deal to buy Supercuts had closed. Proving how quickly paranoia can be helped with the right medicine, she got the franchisees to drop the lawsuit right away. What miracle did she use? The rule of reciprocity.

The franchisees wanted to set up a Supercuts Council, consisting of elected franchisee representatives and company executives, that would meet monthly to discuss problems. The former management refused to even consider it. Burton agreed to it at the very first meeting. Not only that, she insisted that the council meetings be held at corporate headquarters and at corporate expense. If management could instantly agree to such a thing when it hadn't budged in the past, the franchisees figured, they owed Burton one. They were uncomfortable until they reciprocated. So they dropped the lawsuit. That's the rule of reciprocity in action.

This simple treatment for the paranoia bought Burton time to make other changes that would jump-start revenues and increase long-term growth. Before long, Supercuts' paranoia vanished. Within sixteen months, profits were up by 10 percent. Within three years, franchisees logged double-digit sales increases, while revenues grew from $126 million to over $170 million. Growth was back on track too. Supercuts added more than one hundred new franchisees. As one franchisee commented, "My stores are registering record sales and profits. Equally important, people are feeling optimistic about the company. It's nice to be part of something that's heading up again."[4]

4. Mark Stevens, "Turnaround Tricks: Getting a Company Back on Its Feet," *Working Woman*, December 1990, pp. 45–48.

You don't have to be the CEO to use the rule of reciprocity in treating a paranoid organization. You can do it from any position in the company. You'll have to do some advance planning and be prepared when the right opportunity comes.

The first step is to take on something out of the ordinary, something that would not normally be expected as part of your job. It might be serving on a special task force and taking over its leadership when the nominal chair proves ineffective. Perhaps you volunteer to give a speech for your boss if you know she hates doing it. Maybe you find a way to untangle the confusing transmission codes in your company's electronic mail system. Whatever it is, make sure you do an outstanding job of it.

There's a 99 percent likelihood that your supervisor will comment on your good performance. Maybe she'll even say something like "Let me know if we can ever do something for you." But even if all she does is express appreciation, be ready to move right in with the second part of this treatment.

Right there and then, ask permission to take on another project, one that requires a gentle bending of some unwritten rule. The project should be something you are sincerely interested in, and also—this is the key—something that will genuinely benefit the organization. You should already have the project in mind; that's why you must think this process through in advance.

Normally, a manager in a paranoid organization would never permit you to do something if it involved breaking a rule; she's too much in the habit of distrusting everything. But now your boss feels obligated to you, and there's a very good chance she will agree to your request. Once again, do an outstanding job on the project. When your boss thanks you, be ready with yet another request, this time involving another, slightly more serious rule.

The point of all this is to demonstrate, through actual experience, that innovative projects are not by definition dangerous—that you can allow enthusiastic employees to do something slightly unconventional without worrying that they'll stab you in the back. Once managers begin to see these successes, the atmosphere gradually and subtly changes.

Employing Reality Confrontation

Reality confrontation may sound forbidding, but it's not. In essence it means getting the organization to face facts.

There are three elements to reality confrontation: authority, facts, and emotional climate. That is, to get an organization to face reality, a person in authority must present the facts to an audience that is in the right frame of mind to receive them.

Present facts on both sides of an issue; this helps to give you the credibility you need to be convincing. Even those who don't agree with you 100 percent will understand that you are aware of the contrary arguments and are neither ignoring nor attempting to conceal them.

Of course you cannot expect that people will accept facts just because they are true. You must present them in such a way that they are more likely to be received. That is what we mean by creating a climate that is emotionally comfortable. The more difficult the situation, the more important the emotional climate.

How you create this climate depends largely on the situation you are in and whether you are dealing with one person or a group. It may be as simple as moving away from your desk and sitting down side by side with the person. If you are talking to a group, make sure you use the group's language; be extra careful about your own body language, and brush up on your listening skills.

One very effective way to create the right climate is to tell an anecdote or dramatic story that illustrates some of the issues involved in the situation. That is, personalize the facts by showing how a single individual might be affected. This technique is used often by politicians, who tell an anecdote about one person or one family to dramatize the human aspect of the issue.

Let's try this treatment process in a hypothetical situation. Suppose you are the president of a small company that has experienced slowly declining sales for some time now. It is no secret the company is in trouble. Rumors of layoffs are flying around, and people are nervous. There is a sour note of suspicion and distrust in almost all contacts between departments, and productivity has all but disappeared.

You decide to treat this paranoia by getting the organization to confront reality. Call everyone together, if that is practical, and present the facts. Lay out the problem, using illustrations to bring the audience into a receptive climate. Perhaps you tell of companies that went through similar crises and survived: maybe you recount a well-known incident from the company's past. You might talk about hearing your grandfather's stories of the Great Depression, or about your childhood memories of an uncle who was laid off.

Then describe all the alternatives that have been considered, and take the audience through all the pros and cons of each one. Can you avoid layoffs? For the short term, yes. However, the corporation will be unprofitable. You will be unable to borrow money for operations. Massive layoffs are certain to result. So you have reluctantly decided on a fixed percentage of layoffs now. Those let go will be helped to find a new job, and they will have the first shot at jobs when you turn the situation around. Now describe your plan for turning the situation around. Give the best time and number estimates you can.

You may not be popular when you finish this reality confrontation—layoffs are very difficult on everyone in the organization—but you have at least dispelled some of the paranoia. Now that people know what is going to happen, the wild rumors disappear.

Remember that there is one other ingredient of reality confrontation: authority. In our example, the company president has the authority necessary to get an organization to face facts. But what if you are not the organization's top manager? Can you still use reality confrontation? Yes, but usually you must do it on someone else's authority. By way of explanation, let's borrow an idea from sales.

There is an old closing technique known as "The Ben Franklin Close." Salespeople use it when the prospect is fully sold but for some reason can't make the final commitment to buy. The salesperson says something like this: "Wise old Ben Franklin had a method he used to help him make a decision whenever he was faced with a difficult situation like yours. He would write down all the positives on the left side of a sheet of paper, and all the negatives on the right side. Then he would compare the two. Maybe if we did the same in this situation, it would help you in making your decision."

The salesperson then writes each positive and negative in turn and discusses each in detail. This close works because it is a reality confrontation; prospects see what they will gain if they buy and what they will lose if they don't buy. Using Ben Franklin as the authority figure is important. It isn't the salesperson's technique, it is Ben Franklin's.

To use this same concept in reality confrontations, find a way to align your arguments with someone who has stature and credibility with the individuals you are confronting. For instance, you might choose the organization's founder as your surrogate authority. Preface your facts this way: "I remember hearing my father tell about the time Mr. Johnson called the whole company together and told them...." Conclude the anecdote with something like this: "It seems to me that this problem we're dealing with right now is a lot like that one was."

Perhaps there is a person in the organization who everyone thinks was the best boss they ever had. Start by saying, "I was thinking about our problem the other day and trying to imagine what Charlie would do if he were still here." Or compare your situation to a book or article by someone well-known in your field: "I just read a really interesting article in the *Harvard Business Review* about...."

Redirecting

Redirecting means getting an organization to shift its attention to a different direction. The idea is simple: Give organization members something new to think about, to distract them from the paranoia.

Two departments of a company were located next to each other in the same building. Department A was producing a product that the company had been selling for several years; department B was developing a brand-new product. The two departments competed for money and other resources, even in such mundane aspects of their environment as which one got its trash taken out first. Before long, the minor irritations of working so close together developed into low-grade paranoia, a process that was helped along by the manager of department B. Every time he saw people from department A, he chided them for wasting their time on "the boring product." He told his group that the other department's days were definitely numbered. He tried to entice away the best engineers from department A.

Eventually things got so bad that the two departments no longer cooperated on anything. They quit sharing information about technical developments, about manufacturing, about the customer. Neither department trusted the other; people even stopped talking to each other.

The president of this company finally hit on a very simple idea. He didn't know it by name, but his treatment was redirection. He charged both departments with looking for ways to increase efficiency, and then he made his own contribution: He moved department B into its own building. The petty squabbling born of living so close together was gradually replaced by more professional-level competition for company resources. Slowly, the animosity between the two organizations faded, and the paranoia disappeared.

Even if you don't have the authority to move departments around, you can still use redirection to help cure your part of the organization. The essential strategy is the same: Redirect others on a new path that takes them away from the root cause of the paranoia. In the example just cited, workers in either department could have used this treatment. Someone could have suggested a joint project to investigate customer satisfaction of the current product. Anyone could have initiated a redirection toward seeing what parts from the old model might be used in the new. The possibilities are infinite.

Summary

Paranoia—unreasonable suspicion of others' motives—can seriously undermine morale, productivity, and profits. It can be the cause of an organization's losing some of its best talent.

There are four approaches for treating this illness, and they can be used from any position in the organization:

1. Build trust.
2. Use the rule of reciprocity.
3. Employ reality confrontation.
4. Redirect.

6

Fear, Self-Doubt, Paralysis—Neurotic Behavior

Neurosis is the way of avoiding nonbeing by avoiding being.
—Paul Tillich, The Courage to Be

We're all controlled neurotics.
—*Harry Reasoner interview in*
TV Guide, *March 20, 1971*

Neurotic behavior is probably the most prevalent psychological problem in organizations. A neurotic organization is, more than anything else, afraid. But unlike a paranoid organization, it is afraid of itself and doubts its own abilities to cope and succeed. This fear can cause serious problems. Productivity can go into a power dive. Because they are fearful, people in neurotic organizations frequently start spending more time, effort, and resources in trying to avoid failure than in trying to achieve success. This approach ensures minimum success and frequently leads to failure anyway.

As the disease worsens, the neurotic organization begins to doubt itself, and it becomes paralyzed by worry. Eventually, proceeding effectively with any project may become difficult, even impossible. Because of the fear, anxiety, and self-doubt, the organization avoids risk taking and resists changes at any cost. But risk taking is a necessary ingredient of progress. Peter Drucker has observed that the successful organization that continues to do only what it has done in the past is certain to fail eventually. That's because the environment is constantly changing, and the organization must adapt to change with it. So not only is the neurotic organization not going anywhere; it will, unless the illness is arrested, further deteriorate.

The Story of Montgomery Ward

Did you know that before World War II, Montgomery Ward was larger than Sears Roebuck? Today Sears, while it has its problems, is much larger than Montgomery Ward. How did this happen?

Here are the basic facts. Before the war, Montgomery Ward was one of the United States's fastest-growing retail businesses. After the war, it stopped growing. Until 1952, not a single new store was opened. In fact, after the war, twenty-seven stores were closed—every single one of them profitable. Was this crazy? You bet!

Montgomery Ward had become neurotic. Infected by Chairman Sewell Avery's overwhelming fear of postwar financial problems, the entire organization began to dread the future.

Ward could have launched a limited expansion program and still retained large cash reserves. It had plenty of capital on hand to do this. One Ward vice-president even called the company "a bank with a storefront." But the neurotic company knew that poverty was "just around the corner," so it held on to its huge reserves. Not only did Ward cease to expand, it sold assets. Even as the economy expanded, it continued to shrink.

Sears Roebuck retained a cash reserve, too. However, it also put millions of dollars into building new stores. While Sears focused on a vision of becoming America's number one supplier of household goods, Montgomery Ward worried about avoiding failure.[1]

Had you been an employee of Montgomery Ward during this period, you would have noted the following symptoms of neurotic behavior:

- Self-doubt
- Emotional paralysis (inability to act)
- Fear
- Anxiety

Where Neurotic Organizations Go Wrong

The fear of failure that crippled Ward is the most pervasive trait of neurotic companies. That fear leads to several self-defeating behaviors:

- Micromanagement is valued.
- Innovation and risk taking are discouraged.
- Punishing mistakes is applauded.

Let us look at some of the effects of this fearfulness.

Micromanaging

To avoid whatever it is they are afraid of, neurotic organizations fall into the trap of micromanagement: managers' checking and double-checking everything their employees do and making decisions for them every step of the way. The thinking seems to be that if you take care of every little detail, you can prevent failure. Being careful is a good thing, but like all good ideas it can be overdone. When every single manager, up and down the chain, is more concerned with catching mistakes than anything else, the organization is paralyzed by an outbreak of minutiae.

1. Robert F. Hartley, *Marketing Mistakes*, 2nd ed. (Columbus, Ohio: Grid, 1981), pp. 23–34.

If you've ever been part of a micromanaged organization, you know exactly what it's like. In your particular area you may be the expert, but your boss treats you like a complete imbecile, checking and rechecking everything you do and thinking once, twice, and three times before making any decisions. Your natural tendency is to resist this. The more you resist, the more They want to check on you.

They aren't seeking perfection or excellence. They themselves are being checked on, and they're trying to survive. Unfortunately, the root cause of the illness and the fear may be beyond control of most of the company's managers. So managers all the way down the chain of command look over the shoulders of the manager at the next subordinate level. This helps to perpetuate the neurotic behavior and causes the organization to grow increasingly dysfunctional.

Neurotic Behavior Discourages Innovation

Neurotic behavior is especially destructive in organizations that depend on a high degree of innovation and risk taking for their success. While innovation is important to all organizations, those that must spend a lot of time developing new products are especially susceptible to this malady. New product development is risky; as many as nine out of ten new products fail in the marketplace. Healthy organizations know this; they accept failure as a cost of doing business. They also know that the riskiest new products frequently have the highest potential for success.

But neurotic organizations can't face failure; they are too fearful. And this fear paralyzes them. Look what happened at Alpine Engineering Development Company.

Alpine was the market leader in valves for oxygen breathing systems. Through a unique valve invented in the late 1940s, the company dominated its industry for more than twenty years. But Alpine, plagued with the self-doubt that characterizes so many neurotic organizations, was paralyzed with the fear that if it tried to develop a new valve product and failed, it would be exposed as lucky rather than competent. Even while other companies invested resources in a determined effort to develop a new valve, the company took no action. Finally, the inevitable happened: A better valve was developed by someone else. Eventually the company was gobbled up by a competitor.

Search for the Guilty...Punish the Innocent

As we said in the previous section, some degree of failure is inevitable; healthy companies cut their losses and move on. But in neurotic organizations, avoiding failure is more important than achieving success. So when they do have a development failure, they begin a strange process known as "a search for the guilty and the punishment of the innocent." Not only do they punish mistakes, they sometimes punish those who discover the mistakes—the old game of "shoot the messenger."

In their determination to squelch mistakes, neurotic organizations establish rigid rules and policies of supervision that severely handicap any possibility of success. It's the worst kind of vicious circle. With severe restrictions on their creativity, employees of neurotic organizations are unhappy and unproductive; the more creative they are, the more unhappy they become. They also know that their own careers are at risk. Eventually most leave, depriving the organization of the very talents it needs to survive.

Treating the Neurotic Organization

When this disease strikes, you must move quickly to cure it. Here are four techniques that work well:

1. Implementing involvement therapy by using the overload principle
2. Reframing the cause of the behavior
3. Changing the behavior with social pressure
4. Refocusing

Let's look at each of these in turn.

Implementing Involvement Therapy

Involvement therapy means getting someone else involved—more involved than he or she wants to be. That's why the principle underlying this therapy is known as the overload principle.

If your boss wants to look over your shoulder, do more then just let him; encourage him to look even more. Let's say he demands to know everything that you say to anyone about a certain project that you are working on. Great! Prepare a daily contact log. Write down the date, the time, the person you spoke with, the subject, and everything that was discussed. Don't leave out anything. If a secretary says that she is going out to reproduce a copy of a report on this project, give it a complete line item. If a friend mentions something about the project in a different context, give it the same treatment. Overload the system with massive amounts of details. Think of other aspects of the project that you can document.

Attitude is important. Don't be insolent or disrespectful; be friendly and helpful. But always remember that for the short run, keeping the boss informed is your primary mission. If you do this correctly, it won't be long before your boss cries "uncle" and demands that you stop.

Donald Trump tells how the manager of the Grand Hyatt used this technique on him. Trump built the Grand Hyatt and owned a controlling interest. Unfortunately, he became overconcerned with whether the manager was doing his job right; he and his wife interfered with the manager's operations regularly. Of course, the Trumps didn't realize what they were doing. That's always the way in a neurotic organization. When the Trumps wouldn't stop, the manager complained to the head of Hyatt Hotels. The only result was that Trump fired him. Complaining never works in a neurotic organization; it only makes the organization more neurotic.

The new manager of the Grand Hyatt was a lot smarter. As Trump recounts:

The new manager did something brilliant. He began to bombard us with trivia. He'd call up several times a week, and he'd say, "Donald, we want your approval to change the wallpaper on the fourteenth floor" or "We want to introduce a new menu in one of the restaurants" or "We are thinking of switching to a new laundry service." They'd also invite us to all of their management meetings. The guy went so far out of his way to solicit our opinions that I finally said, "Leave me alone, do whatever you want, just don't bother me."[2]

Notice that the second manager caused an overload without getting Trump mad. You can do the same. Simply be friendly and obey the rules, but overload the system at the same time. What if you begin involvement therapy and your boss tells you to work it out on your own? This is a sign of misdiagnosis. Such an occurrence almost never happens in a neurotic company.

Reframing the Cause of the Behavior

You can also alter neurotic behavior by changing the perceptions of those who are ill. This is called reframing and it rests on this fact of human nature: We can look at what we see in more than one way. That's why some see a glass as half-full and others see it as half-empty. In essence, the treatment involves reframing the circumstances of the neurotic behavior to a different point of view.

W. Clement Stone's billion-dollar insurance company was threatened by self-doubt, paralysis, fear, and other symptoms of neurotic behavior. He used a very simple reframing technique built around the philosophy that "for every problem, there is an equal or greater opportunity." He insisted that every executive who came to him with a problem also bring

2. Donald J. Trump and Tony Schwartz, *Trump: The Art of the Deal* (New York: Warner Books, 1987), p. 10.

along an opportunity. Even the founding of his company began with a reframe. The insurance sales organization that he headed became paralyzed when the salespeople learned that the major insurance company for which they sold was going to withdraw its franchise. He reframed the problem as an opportunity for the organization to sell its own insurance.

A small aerospace company in a specialized market started exhibiting signs of neurotic behavior when the defense budget in its area was cut by 80 percent. Many managers didn't know what to do. Some suggested that they immediately initiate layoffs. Others wanted to switch right away to nondefense markets with which they were unfamiliar. People who could find employment in other industries began to leave. Everything was at a neurotic standstill until someone treated the company with reframing. He pointed out that the huge budget cut was driving larger competitors with bigger overheads out of the market. But even 20 percent of the former budget was huge for this small company. So because the budget cut meant reduced competition, it actually represented an opportunity to increase sales!

Big Blue's Reframing

After years of awesome success, IBM suffered some awesome losses. Worse, the fabled organization was beginning to exhibit neurotic tendencies. Fear and self-doubt worked their usual evil.[3] Steve Schwartz, a thirty-three-year veteran at IBM, was named senior vice-president in charge of a new "market-driven quality" program. His assignment: to get rid of the bureaucratic cobwebs and put an end to the defects in IBM's products and processes.

At a meeting with engineers at an IBM plant in Rochester, Massachusetts, Schwartz discovered a peculiar fact. Customer complaints made to the Rochester plant were the same as

3. Thomas Carroll, "Computer Companies Are Launching More Products Than Ever, But Are They Really New?" *Time*, 30 October 1989, p. 72.

those made previously by other users to their local IBM facilities. In a well-run business, one would expect such complaints to be forwarded to headquarters; corporate staff would then alert all local facilities so that the local plants could resolve the problems *before* they received complaints. However, by the time Rochester heard of these complaints, if it heard at all, it was too late: Rochester's own customers had already complained. Besides the sheer stupidity of waiting for the customer to complain, correcting some of these complaints was causing major expenses. That these costs were unnecessary was particularly disturbing. Digging deeper, Schwartz saw that the same was true at all IBM plants. IBM managers considered customer complaints a local problem.

So Schwartz reframed the situation. He proclaimed that local customer complaints would no longer be considered a local plant problem. From then on, any customer complaint was a *company* problem. He put software engineers to work designing a program that would coordinate this information. Now employees at individual branch offices all over the United States log in complaints on their own computers and zap them off electronically to a central computer at headquarters; from there, the complaints go to all IBM branches and plants. With this centralized data, the company can anticipate many problems and solve them before customers even see them.[4] Clearly, this one treatment didn't cure IBM. IBM is still being treated as this is written. But reframing was and *is* part of the treatment.

This did not miraculously solve all IBM's problems. As we write, the company still struggles with staggering losses; it has announced new layoffs, reduced stock dividends, and replaced its chairperson. But that does not diminish what Schwartz accomplished: With reframing techniques, he changed the perception of the environment and eliminated the neurotic behavior. In the process he saved a lot of money and effort for IBM and made customers happy.

4. Barbara Hetzer, "Impossible Mission, Unflappable Boss," *Business Month*, October 1990.

Changing the Behavior With Social Pressure

Social pressure is people power: the persuasive force exerted
on a group by the will, personality, or charisma of some of its
members. If that pressure is strong enough, anything is possible. The group will believe what might otherwise be unbeliev-
able, or it might take extraordinary actions. Social pressure is
what makes kids take drugs—or decide it is "cool" to *not* use
drugs. Lynch mobs are the result of social pressure. So are the
demonstrations that won civil rights for minorities in the
United States. Clearly, social pressure is a force that can be
used for either good or evil. You can use it to dissipate
neurotic behavior and inoculate the organization against future attacks.

An interesting experiment in psychology shows us a great
deal about social pressure. A group of volunteers is asked to
watch certain people make a statement and then decide whether
the statement is true or false. One at a time, presenters enter
the room, make their statement, and then leave. All the
observers then say whether they think the person was lying or
telling the truth; a recorder notes each observer's opinion.

In reality, the true purpose of the experiment was to
determine to what extent each observer could be influenced
by the others. When the majority of observers concluded that
a particular presenter had lied, all the others agreed with that
conclusion, even if the person had been telling the truth.
Their conclusions were based not so much on the actual
presentation as on the expressed opinions of their peers.

Social pressure can come from many different kinds of
groups. These include family, friends, peers, and other groups
that share some commonality of interest and that have influence on those in the organization. But generally, social pressure is most effective if it springs from within the organization
itself.

A small private college became neurotic when recession
caused enrollment to drop. All sorts of promotions to increase
applications were tried, with little effect. Talk spread that
layoffs might be necessary, even among older staff and tenured
faculty. Everyone was paralyzed with fear and self-doubt; no

one seemed to be able to do anything. Enrollments continued to fall.

Then one day a young professor happened to comment to an older colleague, "Well, what difference does it make how many students we have or what happens in the future? Are we not educators today?"

The older man stood stock still. He turned to the young professor and smiled. "I think you have something there."

"Are we not educators?" became a rallying cry whenever anyone voiced pessimism. The words implied faith in the profession and in the institution, and this faith created a tremendous social pressure for positive action. Everyone became something of a fanatic. The result was quality education for the current "customers" and a host of new programs. Faculty and students alike went into aggressive fund raising. At first the neurotic behavior disappeared. Then the unusual activity at the university caught the attention of the press. Enrollment increased, first in a trickle and then in a torrent. While other schools downsized because of the recession, this school expanded. Social pressure can be powerful medicine!

Even outsiders can plant the seeds of social pressure. The president of one company, who hadn't had a vacation in years, took a two-month trip to Europe. During his absence, the union representing many of his employees became neurotic. Misinterpreting some of his previous actions, it convinced the membership that immediate action was necessary. While the president was still on vacation, the union struck with no warning.

Naturally, the president took the first plane back. Even by then, the union doubted its own actions. Clearly, it had made a mistake, but what could it do? To call off the strike with no negotiations or benefits won would look ridiculous. Leaders and membership alike were paralyzed.

The president realized that the actions of the union were irrational. He decided to handle the situation by doing something unexpected: addressing the immediate needs of striking employees. He ordered a free child care center for the children of striking members so spouses could work. He made baseball and other sports equipment available for employees not actually on the picket line, and he set aside a company lot so they could play. He had refreshments brought out to those who were picketing. Soon the members felt better about management than about their own leaders. They began to pressure the union leadership for a quick and amicable settlement. Social pressure from the membership changed the union's neurotic behavior.

One important lesson here is that you do not even need to be a member of an organization to change the organization's behavior. What you do need to do is to use the right psychological tool in the right way.

Refocusing

Another tactic for treating the neurotic organization is to distract it from the fear that it feels. You do this by getting it to focus on something else.

You may have seen Joe Sugarman, president of JS&A, advertising his popular products on television. His multimillion-dollar company is now well-established. But twenty years ago, it almost died before it got off the ground.

Back in 1972, Joe pioneered the sale of hand-held calculators by mail order. His first mailing, to 50,000 accountants, was a flop. His investment organization, fearing more failure, wanted him to fold. But Joe knew something the organization didn't: The cost of the calculator was about to drop by 25 percent.

So, armed with the knowledge of which mailing lists worked and which didn't, he confronted the investment organization and got it to refocus on the potential for profit instead of the potential for failure. The next mailing was to 400,000. Sugarman tells what happened next:

"There were more responses than I could possibly handle—more, in fact, than I could possibly imagine."[5] No wonder we keep seeing Joe on TV today.

5. Joseph Sugarman, *Success Forces* (Chicago: Contemporary Books, 1980), pp. 69–73.

Summary

Neurotic behavior is mostly about self-doubt and fear of failure. It causes organizational paralysis. Take these actions to treat any organization for its neurotic behavior:

1. If neurotic behavior is present, don't delay. Start action to cure it right away. You may believe it will get better on its own. It won't. It will only get worse.
2. Use involvement therapy. Overload the system by happily and pleasantly doing whatever the organization demands, but doing it to such an extent that the organization can't take it.
3. Change the organization's behavior by changing its perception of what it sees as a threat. In other words, reframe the "threat."
4. Use social pressure to dampen the neurotic behavior.
5. Get the organization to focus on something other than the fear it feels.

Chapter 7

"Why Bother Trying?"—Depression

Depression is our epidemic emotional illness.
—*Webster Scott*, The New York Times,
March 16, 1975

Being in an organization that suffers from depression is, well, depressing. All around you are people who are indifferent, apathetic, lethargic. They seem to have no energy, and no emotion. They show no interest in the future, no commitment to the company's past. Moreover, the depressed company knows it is depressed. It feels guilty over this and over not doing better in whatever it is doing. It wishes it could just give up.

Tragically, the diminished capacity of the depressed organization to mobilize its employees and resources toward a common goal and to become productive adds to its depressed state. The organization suffering this malady is on a downward spiral. Without help, it is headed for massive failure. Unless it is cured of its illness, its competitors or the market will mercifully kill it off.

During the conflict in Vietnam, many companies got involved in the development or production of body armor. This product gave soldiers and airmen some protection from fragments of exploding shells. With half a million men and women in Vietnam, there was a strong demand. However, when U.S. troops withdrew, this demand vanished.

Most companies quickly switched to more profitable products. Many prospered by taking their knowledge to other fields. Some entered the market for police body armor, which was just beginning to grow. One company didn't shift at all. It subsisted on the little work that remained. This company became smaller and smaller. It refused to seriously consider new markets or new products.

Outsiders entering this once-thriving company felt as if they were entering a morgue. The workplace was deadly quiet. Employees silently shuffled from one place to another. Suggestions for a change were met by faint smiles. "We're just not very good at doing anything else" was the standard answer. "We've tried a couple of other things, but we haven't been able to get it together." Finally there was no work and the company went out of business.

In depressed companies you'll note the following symptoms:

- Little energy
- Apathy
- A lack of initiative
- A lack of commitment
- Guilt
- The desire to give up

Treating the Depressed Organization

Treating a depressed organization involves three required steps:

1. First, distract the organization from its depression by getting it to focus on something else.
2. Then give the organization something to feel good about.
3. Finally, build the organization's confidence by giving it a real victory.

Let's examine how several companies put the process to work.

Driving Porsche to Victory

Peter Schutz, an American, broke a cycle of organizational depression when he took over Porsche in 1980. Soon after Schutz came on board, he was told that the company had decided not to race at Le Mans, the prestigious European auto race. Commanded Schutz, "I don't care what you have to do, but Porsche is going to win at Le Mans." Schutz himself not only accompanied the team to Le Mans but spent the entire time in the pits. When Porsche won, that victory helped lift the depression. And as one engineer commented, it proved that Schutz was the right man for Porsche.[1]

Treating the Donahue Manufacturing Company

The affable president of the Donahue Manufacturing Company had worked himself up through the sales department. At least once a week he stopped by the sales department to see "his boys." "How much money have you fellows made for me today?" he would ask, chortling. And they would laugh back at him, saying, "Not enough for you, we know, but more than enough."

The salespeople loved the attention, for they had great confidence in their president. They felt that his very presence was lucky. As long as they saw his name on the door, they were convinced that they were unbeatable.

Then President Donahue retired. Almost immediately, sales began to fall. The sales manager saw that his people were making fewer sales calls. They had become afraid; they believed that with Donahue's retirement they had lost their luck. In this case, as in so many others, perception was reality.

1. Craig R. Hickman and Michael A. Silva, *Creating Excellence* (New York: New American Library, 1984), pp. 26–27.

Fewer sales calls meant fewer sales. Fewer sales led to depression and a lack of confidence, which led to still fewer sales calls: the downward spiral of depression. Soon the salespeople were so depressed they couldn't sell anything. All they could do was take orders.

The sales manager understood the problem. He even explained it to his subordinates. But try as he might, he could not improve the situation. Then one day he had an idea.

He called the sales organization together, but he didn't say anything about sales calls. In fact, he didn't mention sales at all. Instead he asked, "How many here have ever jumped out of an airplane?" No one raised a hand. "I'm told," he continued, "that skydiving is lots of fun." He had their interest now. "I've never jumped out of an airplane," he continued, "but I might like to. Who here would be willing to make a parachute jump with me if the company pays for training, insurance, and one parachute jump?"

After they realized that the sales manager wasn't joking, the salespeople jumped in with questions and comments. It was the longest discussion they had ever had on any subject. Someone asked why the company would pay for them to go skydiving. "Oh, I don't know," he answered. "I guess the new boss just wants to know if we've got the stomach for it." At last, of thirty-one salespeople, sixteen agreed to accept the challenge.

Note that the manager didn't once mention declining sales or sales calls. His unusual proposal distracted his employees from their depression. They refocused on the challenge of jumping from an airplane.

Two weeks later, fourteen of the sixteen salespeople actually showed up, completed their training, and jumped. Five more jumped a week later, and three more the week after that. Now the salespeople started to feel good about themselves. They felt they were special. No other sales force they knew jumped out of airplanes. In fact, they were hard pressed to think of anyone in the whole industry who did it.

Then a wonderful thing happened: Confidence returned. The salespeople felt that if they could jump out of an airplane, they could do anything. They began making more sales calls;

in fact, they made more calls than they had before the president retired. As they made more sales calls, they made more sales. From these victories, their confidence returned, and the number of calls and sales increased even more. Strangely, calls and sales increased even among those who did not jump. They caught the spirit from those who had. This confirmed that the depression was an organizational ailment.

Using the Three Steps at Texaco

Taking dramatic action gets the depressed organization onto a different track and allows it to break out of a depressed cycle. Fortunately, there are other ways to distract an organization besides jumping out of airplanes. Many other actions, some quite simple, can get the organization focused on something else.

Depressed organizations tend to get caught in a sort of mental rut that sustains the depression. If you can interrupt this pattern, that one action will provide the necessary distraction and break the state of depression. At Texaco, one man did it with a speech.

In 1984, Texaco, Inc., was sued by Pennzoil and lost. The court ordered Texaco to pay Pennzoil $11.1 billion in damages; shortly thereafter, Texaco filed for bankruptcy. Three years later, James W. Kinnear took over as CEO. The company still wasn't out of bankruptcy, and management was forced to expend much of its energy and scarce resources fighting off takeovers.[2] Compared with other oil companies, Texaco ranked dead last in almost every category. Not surprisingly, morale was pretty low. Kinnear took charge of a deeply depressed organization.

He started his treatment by doing something totally unexpected. He announced that he planned to address the entire company, and he notified Texaco offices all around the world of the time and date. Thanks to the use of modern communications technology, every single Texaco employee worldwide

2. "Corporate Raiders: Icahn's $340 Million Payoff," *Time*, 13 February 1989, p. 63.

would hear the speech. The employees thought they knew what was coming: criticism, announcement of more cutbacks, admonishments to work harder and be more productive.

Wrong. In his speech, Kinnear congratulated them on the way they had handled the pressure of the previous years. "You ought to be proud of yourselves," he said. Kinnear promised his employees that their fortitude would be rewarded soon. And he went on to outline his vision for the company's future.

Kinnear then implemented step two: he created situations where people could win. These were minor successes in specially targeted markets. These wins were easily achieved, and they had their desired effect: Texaco employees felt more confident. They felt good about themselves.

With some minor success under its belt, the organization was set up for the final part of the treatment: a major victory. This came with the introduction of a new gasoline additive called System 3. Developing this new product required a major company investment and was not without risk. But System 3 won customer acceptance. By 1989, Texaco's depression was past. The company posted a $2.4 billion profit.[3]

Getting a Manufacturer Back in Shape

Now let's watch a smaller organization use the same technique. A small manufacturer of bodybuilding equipment ran into some development problems with its high-technology line. It had intended to be first in the market with a device using hydraulic valves for resistance; instead it was a distant third. As a result, sales were far short of forecasts, and the company went into a deepening depression.

The employees were worried about layoffs. The president gave them something else to be upset about: He mandated that until further notice all employees would be required to come to work an hour early. In this hour, they would work out, under supervision, using the equipment they built. Even

3. "A Winning Vision: Selling Your Way Back From Disaster," *Success*, May 1990, p. 14.

the bodybuilders among the employees found this distasteful, since it disrupted their own regular workout schedules. Employees complained bitterly, some threatened to quit. However, the unpopular action had an important effect: It interrupted the organization's depressed state and gave the president time to work on a new marketing plan.

First, however, the president got the organization into phase two: feeling good about itself. He started a new compensation plan in which improvements in physical fitness, measured objectively, resulted in salary bonuses. Several employees qualified right away as a sole result of the daily mandatory workouts.

The new marketing plan focused on a market niche the company had not considered previously: the institutional market. As the company moved into implementing the plan, the mandatory exercise was dropped. Phase three was complete as the company captured a major share of this new market.

Taking Care of Yourself

When you are part of an organization that suffers from a psychological disorder, and you hope to promote change, it is important for you to take extra steps to protect your own emotional well-being. You cannot be an effective agent for change if you get sucked into the illness. This is true of all the nine illnesses, but it is especially true of depression.

In Chapter 12, we describe several techniques for creating what we have called the "sphere of wellness."

Summary

To cure a depressed organization, you must break the cycle of depression by using three steps:

1. Distract the organization from its depression.
2. Give it something to feel good about.
3. Give it a victory.

Chapter 8

Insecurity Masked With Addiction— Intoxication

They are drunken, but not with wine; they stagger, but not with strong drink.

—Isaiah 29:9

Every form of addiction is bad, no matter whether the narcotic be alcohol or morphine or idealism.

—Carl Gustav Jung

If you are familiar with the behavior of an alcoholic or drug abuser, you can understand a company afflicted with intoxication. The intoxicated organization is drunk. It is addicted to something. Even though deep down it knows that the addiction is harmful, it generally refuses to recognize that it has a problem. If confronted, it usually reacts with denial.

The intoxicated organization, even more than those with other illnesses, is unwilling or unable to examine its sickness dispassionately. It refuses to face potential problem issues, regardless of how intensely or passionately they are predicted. It completely closes its eyes and its ears to warnings from inside or outside the organization. This organization won't be confused by the facts. It tells itself that everything is going well, even in the face of repeated failures.

Surprisingly, morale is often high. Employees say, in effect, "Everything is fine. We're doing great!" That sounds a bit like mania. And indeed there is some surface resemblance between mania and intoxication, principally in this high-flying enthusiasm.

But there is one important difference. Manic organizations genuinely think they are invincible; they believe they can accomplish anything. Intoxicated organizations may *seem* confident, but look closer and you will see insecurity and self-doubt. This is really the key to understanding intoxication: The organization becomes intoxicated to mask these shortcomings from itself. Intoxication permits the organization to forget faults that would be known and understood if the organization were sober. But it's a poor exchange. Eventually, uncorrected problems lead to catastrophe. Like intoxicated people who believe they are invincible when high on alcohol or drugs, an intoxicated organization is bound to run into serious trouble sooner or later.

In an intoxicated company you'll find:

- Inability to do a self-analysis
- Self-doubt
- Insecurity
- Addiction

Intoxication at Tailhook '91

There is a real danger that members of an intoxicated organization will come to feel they have no responsibility to question anything that occurs in their environment. They no longer see themselves as accountable for critically analyzing decisions and events. They reach the point where they simply go along with whatever seems normal in the organization. This was the real tragedy of the 1991 Tailhook scandal.

The Tailhook Association is a private group with close ties to the U.S. Navy; its members are active-duty and retired naval aviators, and its activities are officially supported by the navy. Its annual convention, which has been held at the Las Vegas Hilton for some twenty years, attracts not only association members but also senior naval officers, members of Congress, and representatives from private industry.

We now know that over the years conduct at the convention had increasingly grown out of hand. On the third floor, known as the "third deck," numerous hospitality suites featured heavy drinking, strippers, and prostitutes. In 1986, convention attendees dreamed up a new tradition: the "gauntlet." They lined the halls of the third floor, trapping women as they got off the elevator and grabbing, fondling, and forcibly disrobing them. At the 1991 convention, one of the women assaulted happened to be a naval officer herself, an admiral's aide. And she went public with her story.

In intoxicated organizations, it is all too easy for those who should know better to rationalize the facts. And that is what happened here. Senior officers generally expressed the notion that this was just a case of "boys being boys." When the aide reported the incident to her superior, the admiral, his response was, "What did you expect, getting involved with a group of drunken aviators?" A year later, the rationalization continued. Testifying to Congress on another matter in 1992, the chief of staff of the air force was asked about the scandal. "What happened at Tailhook," he replied, "was something that you might expect of a bunch of lieutenants who get together and have too much to drink."[1]

Investigation into the 1991 incident revealed that the behavior had been known about, and condoned, for years. In the shakeout that followed, the secretary of the navy was forced to resign, and the admiral who had rebuked his aide was severely disciplined.

But how did this happen in the first place? How could an organization of intensely trained, highly disciplined individuals fall into this clearly unhealthy behavior?

The Tailhook Association case is almost a classic example

1. Melissa Healy, "U.S. Military Chiefs Oppose Combat Roles for Women," *Los Angeles Times*, 31 July 1992, pp. A-1, A-20.

of the intoxicated organization. It has very little to do with the fact that the offenders were themselves physically intoxicated. Remember that the root cause of intoxication is self-doubt and insecurity. At first it may seem incongruous to suggest that naval aviators, with hundreds of hours of hazardous flying experience, could be troubled by self-doubt and insecurity. Yet we believe that is exactly the case.

The incident occurred when all the armed services were under considerable pressure to allow women to serve in combat, including combat aviation. This is an inflammatory issue with many military people. Combat is one of the last great bastions of the male warrior, and combat aviators are the elite of the military services. Many who choose to fly combat aircraft do so at least partly for the macho image. For their part, the services do everything possible to maintain the image and the mystique; they believe that this increases male bonding and contributes to combat effectiveness. Male service members, particularly aviators, are psychologically dependent on their combat image; the possibility that women could do the same job is very threatening to them. That kind of insecurity led, we believe, to the intoxication that afflicted the Tailhook organization.

It is perhaps extremely relevant that during the 1991 convention, on the very day of the infamous incident, more than a thousand aviators attended an afternoon seminar in which they were able to ask questions of naval leaders. A woman pilot asked why women couldn't fly in combat. Audience response was highly emotional. Tapes of the incident reveal catcalls, ridicule, and anger. Authorities in attendance looked at each other sheepishly. Failure even to try to control the intoxication that erupted in the meeting probably contributed to what happened later that evening.

Intoxication at Apple

Intoxication is especially rampant among entrepreneurial companies that grow large quickly. Witness what happened at Apple Computer.

Although a company with a dazzling record of success, Apple had an unfortunate tendency toward intoxication. The intoxication showed up in the bizarre belief that Apple knew what the customer wanted better than the customer did. This cavalier attitude covered up some massive insecurities. Neither Steve Jobs nor Steve Wozniak, Apple's young founders, had ever finished college; neither had a technical or managerial background from a senior position in a major corporation. These two talented "kids," only a couple of years out of high school, built a billion-dollar corporation out of someone's garage. Now a huge corporation, Apple faced major competition, including such giants as IBM, in the personal computer market. It was a market that Apple had built, but it was now saturated.

Apple responded by introducing a new product, the Lisa model. Lisa was designed as a closed box that couldn't be opened without a special tool. "That way, people can't screw it up," the company reasoned. Apple also decided that if customers did open the computer, it would void the owner's warranty. Other interesting decisions were made: a high price ($10,000) and inoperative cursor keys that forced buyers to use the mouse. As John Sculley, the new chairman, later recalled, "Steve (Jobs) would decide what people needed."[2] People decided otherwise. Apple profits tumbled 80 percent, and stock fell from $63 to $23 a share.

Treating this setback as an aberration, Apple continued in its intoxication. Two years later, the Macintosh was introduced. The early model couldn't hook up to other computers. Customers had said they wanted networks, but Apple thought otherwise. When questioned, senior Apple executives responded with answers typical of the intoxicated: "Don't worry"; "trust me"; "this is the way we've always done it"; "we know what we're doing."

They didn't. Apple thought it could sell 80,000 to 100,000 Macs a month; instead, it sold fewer than 20,000. Before the crisis ended, Apple lost $2.5 billion (that's *billion* with a *b*) and Steve Jobs lost his company.

2. John Sculley, *Odyssey* (New York: Harper & Row, 1987), p. 163.

Ironically, another well-known company predated Apple's intoxication in almost the same way. In the 1920s, Ford customers complained about the limited choice of colors for Ford automobiles. Henry Ford, another self-made man, retorted, "Customers can have any color car they wish . . . so long as it's black." Ford changed its policy after thousands of customers switched to General Motors.

Treating the Intoxicated Organization

Fortunately, harmful as intoxication can be, there are powerful treatments available. Here are three we've used with success.

1. Confrontation after rapport
2. Past-present-future therapy
3. Impact therapy

Confronting After Building Rapport

Confronting the organization with its intoxication is the single best treatment for the disease. The problem is that this is never easy. Few want to listen to someone who claims that the organization has an intoxication problem. Reality confrontation of the sort used for treating paranoia (see Chapter 5) is unlikely to work here. The intoxicated organization is so out of phase with normal behavior that the patient won't pay any attention to the rational approach to confrontation. To get anyone to listen, you must first establish rapport.

Rapport means a relationship of harmony, affinity, and accord. Consider the following experience: You listen to someone you disagree with. Your disagreement may be violent. Still, that person wins you over. If you think back to what was said, you probably don't even remember. What you do recall is the wonderful rapport with this other person. Similarly, have you ever gotten angry when someone told you something that wouldn't anger you at all had you heard it from someone else? Why does this occur? We accept statements from a person with whom we are in rapport that we would not accept from someone else.

Fortunately, there is an easy and reliable way you can gain rapport with anyone. It works even with someone you've just met, even if you apparently have nothing at all in common. And it works almost instantaneously.

This "wonder" technique is called mirroring. It means that when you are talking with a person you want to build rapport with, you match your actions to the other person's behaviors. You use the same words that person uses, speaking in similar tempo and tone of voice. You match your breathing to the person's. You mirror that person's movement and body posture.

How you do this is important. Make gradual adjustment in your behavior. Don't suddenly and abruptly change everything you do to mimic the other, or that person will feel ridiculed. Slowly, bit by bit, begin to change your voice so it sounds more like the other person's. Slowly adjust your rate and depth of breathing. Incorporate her phrases and statements into your comments, using her vocabulary. Slowly, without being abrupt or obvious, copy the other person's actions. If she scratches her nose with her right hand, you scratch your nose with your right hand. If she crosses her right leg over her left, you do the same. If she sits up straight, you sit up straight. If she slouches, you slouch too. But don't react instantly; try to follow actions and changes slowly and naturally.

Scientists don't know exactly why mirroring works, but it does work. It appears to trigger a psychomechanism in our body that tells us we can trust someone who appears to be like us. And this mechanism seems to depend more on visual and auditory cues than on processing of word meanings by the brain.

Mirroring is a one-on-one technique. If you believe you see symptoms of intoxication in your organization, figure out who is in the best position to take remedial action, and try to talk to that person. In your face-to-face meeting, use mirroring to establish rapport so that the other person is more likely to hear what you have to say. You may have to meet with several people, one at a time. If you are able to convince a senior manager that intoxication exists, the ripple effect will take over, and reality will spread throughout the organization.

Using Past-Present-Future Therapy

Do you remember how the ghosts of Christmas past, present, and future took Scrooge on trips during the night of Christmas Eve in Dickens's famous story? You can use the same concept to force organizations to face the future results of undesirable present actions.

An American importer who was searching in Japan for new products met a young man on a street corner selling watercolor prints for three dollars each. The importer thought the product would be a potential big seller in the United States, and through his interpreter he asked how much the prints would be if he bought ten thousand a month.

The interpreter reported, "He says that if you buy ten thousand a month, the price will be five dollars each."

"There must be some mistake. He must have misunderstood. Ask him again."

The interpreter spoke to the print seller in Japanese again and then turned to the American. "He says, if you want ten thousand every month, he wants five dollars each. He says that he has a small factory at home. His workers only complete one thousand a month now. If he has to sell you ten thousand a month, he will have to open a larger factory. He will have to hire more people. He will have to buy more materials. He says he will have many additional problems. So he wants an additional two dollars each."

What do we see here? Symptoms of self-doubt and insecurity. The vendor was addicted to a limited concept of how prints must be sold: a case of mild intoxication.

Through the interpreter, the importer treated the print seller as deftly as the ghosts treated Scrooge. He started by talking about the dreams that the vendor had had when he first started the print business. Making some astute guesses, the importer painted a picture that many ambitious young men have: acquiring wealth, importance, and beautiful things. Then with some quick mental calculation, he estimated the vendor's current income and contrasted his current semipoverty with the earlier dreams. Finally, he talked to the seller about his future. If he continued selling only one thousand prints a month, what would he have when he became old? He would be no wealthier. He would not be any better off than he was today. His wife would be no better off. His children would be uneducated and as poor as he, condemned to the same life, maybe even the same way of earning a living.

This treatment for intoxication was very painful to the print seller, but it worked. The American may have treated the Japanese vendor out of his own self-interest. However, he cured him of intoxication in the process.

Past-present-future therapy works because it forces the organization to recognize the painful results that the intoxicated state can lead to. Presenting the whole story, from past through present to future, creates a compelling forum for making your point.

How you use this therapy in your organization depends largely on your position. If you are in charge, you might gather your group for an informal talk. If you are in a lower position, you might find it more effective to prepare a written report for your manager. If your concern is for the entire organization but you are not in authority, ask to make a formal presentation to the management committee. Then go all out with graphics, stories, and data projections, making your case as dramatic as the situation permits. In all cases, your goal is to break the state of intoxication and leave the corporate patient open to change.

Using Impact Therapy

Impact therapy is similar to past-present-future therapy. Both treat the organization by shocking the patient out of its intoxication. With impact therapy, you create a momentary trauma that breaks the intoxicated state. This causes the organization to stop, look, and think about its actions. Since the trauma is transitory, it will dissipate on its own.

During the Cold War, the Strategic Air Command (SAC) was the organization charged with the awesome responsibility for nuclear retaliation. Standards were extremely high. Bombing accuracy, from even a thirty-thousand-foot altitude, was measured in a few feet. Flight crews had to meet time schedules within minutes, even after flying for several thousand miles. Daily training to high standards and unannounced inspections throughout the year kept all units at the peak of readiness to carry out a war mission, if necessary.

One highly ranked bomber wing had never failed an inspection in its twelve years of existence. It was the only unit in SAC that had won the Fairchild Trophy during annual bombing competition three times. During the Cuban missile crisis, it maintained its aircraft on air or ground alert at a higher rate than any other unit.

Over a period of time, this organization became intoxicated with its own success. The unit developed an attitude. "Why work so hard when we're unbeatable anyway?" Training standards began to slip. The organization ignored these training results as insignificant. One day an unannounced inspection team flew in, and the entire unit was tested as it simulated its war mission. When the results came in, crews and support personnel alike were surprised to discover that they had failed. Still intoxicated with their previous success, they decided that the failure was just a fluke. They knew they would be retested three months later.

One evening several days later, a U.S. Air Force jet appeared without warning in the traffic pattern. No flight plan had been filed at the unit's base. The pilot requested and received permission to land. When the pilot alighted from the plane, he announced himself as the new wing commander. He immediately fired the officer commanding runway security for not isolating a potentially hostile aircraft on the ground until its identity had been confirmed. As the new commander made his way to the command post, the word was quickly passed around: Beware of an unfamiliar colonel. He was firing about half the officers he ran into on his way from the runway!

This was impact therapy at its best. It instantly broke the organization out of its intoxicated state.

The new commander demanded a level of performance that many thought impossible. A few older, slower flyers retired from the air force. The new commander said that he would transfer anyone that wanted out; a few took him up on his offer. But those who stayed were no longer intoxicated. The unit soon performed to its capabilities, a fact reflected in daily bomb scores and other aspects of routine training. And it passed its remake inspection with the highest score ever attained. After the organization returned to normal, and proved it by its actions, the colonel eased off his impact therapy treatment.

This episode shows us two things about applying impact therapy in business. First, it can only be done by the person at the top of the organization, because only that person has the power to create the necessary impact. That doesn't mean you have to be the president of the company, but it does mean you have to be in charge of your subunit. Remember, though, wellness in any organization, no matter how tiny, tends to spread.

Second, it is best if you administer this therapy when you are new to the organization—an unknown quantity. The combination of the unknown and the impact therapy itself greatly increases the power of the treatment.

You can use impact therapy when you have been an organization's manager for some time, but we don't recommend it in most instances. If you use impact therapy by making a major change in your management style, or if you increase performance demands significantly and with no warning, you are going to have problems. Some in the organization may fail to take you seriously. Impact therapy under these circumstances may cause resentment, disciplinary problems, and other troubles that you must deal with in addition to the intoxication. However, in extreme situations in which other treatments have failed, the risks of this happening may need to be taken.

Using Perceptual Contrast to Make Treatments More Effective

Organizations change more readily, no matter what treatment you use, when the change appears easy. This is especially true with the disease of intoxication, which is based on self-doubt and insecurity. An organization that has doubts about its ability to do something is more likely to attempt the task if it seems easy. Similarly, an insecure organization is more likely to change if the change seems slight. Therefore, when you are dealing with an intoxicated organization, it helps if you can get the organization to perceive the necessary change as something smaller than it actually is.

You can do this through the principle of perceptual contrast. Simply stated, perceptual contrast has to do with a basic fact of human psychology. We evaluate things by comparing them with other, similar things; the contrast makes each seem more different than if we had experienced it by itself. Hand a person a glass of water. After he puts it down, hand him a pitcher of water. The pitcher will appear far heavier than if the person had not lifted a glass of water first.

How can this help us with our treatment of intoxication? Consider the Japanese print seller. At first, the contrast principle was working against the importer. The print seller was comparing his current troubles with those he would have if the number of prints increased. The American forced him to compare his earlier dreams with his dismal present, which make the present and future appear far worse than they were. The importer could have increased effectiveness of the past-present-future therapy by also talking about companies successfully producing 100,000 prints a month. Then when he mentioned the 10,000 figure again, it would have seemed much smaller.

Summary

Although in some respects the illness of intoxication resembles mania, the two are different. On one level the intoxicated organization knows that the sources of intoxication are bad for it, but it ignores the danger and often denies it. So we cannot use the same treatments as for mania. The therapies we use to treat intoxication are:

1. Confrontation after rapport
2. Past-present-future therapy
3. Impact therapy

It's important to remember that confrontation should be used with the intoxicated organization only after you gain rapport. An organization suffering from intoxication is too out of phase to accept your confrontation unless rapport has been achieved first. Finally, you can increase the effectiveness of your therapies through the use of perceptual contrast.

Chapter 9

"It's Not Perfect Yet"—
Obsessive Compulsion

I was seized by the stern hand of Compulsion, that dark, unseasonable Urge that impels women to clean house in the middle of the night.

—James Thurber *in* There's a Time for Flags

That fellow seems to me to possess but one idea, and that is the wrong one.

—Samuel Johnson *in James Boswell's*
The Life of Samuel Johnson, LL.D. *(1770)*

Psychologists use the term *obsession* to describe thoughts that a person cannot stop thinking and *compulsion* to describe actions that a person cannot stop doing. Often they go together, and then we say a person suffers from obsessive compulsion. That sounds pretty formidable, but it's easier to understand if we break it into parts. We know what we mean when we say someone is obsessed with something: The person can't stop thinking about it; those thoughts keep coming back to mind, to an unhealthy degree. We also know what we mean by *compulsion*; it's something habitual that you just *have* to do, over and over, even if it doesn't make a lot of sense.

In people, this illness can produce bizarre behavior. In organizations, it produces an unreasonable, unhealthy focus on one thing. Most of the time, that one thing is the relentless pursuit of perfection.

The Acton Metals Company hired Joe Edgar away from a much larger company. In his previous job, he had implemented a total-quality program with much success, cutting manufacturing costs by 18 percent and significantly reducing customer complaints. Acton gave Joe a vice-presidency, and he lost no time setting up a number of programs that had worked well at his previous company. He created a new slogan—"Seek Perfection Daily"—and posted it on every wall. Continual progress toward perfection was expected; quality measurements were taken every month and reported to top management.

Unfortunately, every now and then someone goofed. Employees soon discovered that mistakes were considered unacceptable in the new environment. They quickly figured out that the best way to minimize mistakes was to minimize risk. "Perfection" was sought by avoiding or postponing any decision making that implied risk.

After two years, the company was a full-blown obsessive-compulsive. Joe's measurements confirmed that, indeed, the number of errors had declined. Unfortunately, employee morale, profits, and market share also had dropped.

You wouldn't need to look too closely at Acton Metals to see:

- A strong need for perfection; work never good enough
- Punishment of mistakes
- A tendency to postpone or avoid decision making

Although the quest for perfection is probably the most frequent form that the illness takes in organizations, it isn't the only one. We know of one company that was obsessed with physical fitness. Practically every manager was a marathon runner. The company sponsored a number of physical fitness activities and strongly encouraged all workers to take part. Whereas physical fitness is desirable, in this company it took priority over everything else. Hiring and promotion had less to do with how well employees could do their jobs and more to do with their physical prowess. Each employee had personal fitness goals to achieve, and anything less than 100 percent brought negative consequences. This company finally ran into problems. While its executives were setting physical fitness records, its competitors were satisfying customers. Only a costly turnaround saved it. Most of its former managers were forced to leave the company. We must admit, though, that with few exceptions, all were in very good shape and looked terrific.

Obsessive-Compulsive Managers

It is not always true that a psychological ailment begins with the managers at the very top of an organization; most of the illnesses described in this book can start just about anywhere. In theory, even obsessive compulsion could start at any level. In actuality, though, it often starts with the boss. That is because the person in charge has the power to enforce this demand for perfection. If that person is obsessive-compulsive by temperament, he or she can impose that behavior on the entire organization, whether that be a work unit, a department, or the whole company.

Obsessive-compulsive managers are usually perfectionists. They are so preoccupied with details that nothing is ever good enough. Every project, no matter how large or small, is checked and rechecked. Because it has to be done over and over again, work is almost always late. These managers have a hard time making decisions, because every decision has to be perfect. The results of all this obsession with perfection are delays, wasted resources, lowered morale, and, not infrequently, the very calamity that the manager was trying to avoid.

That's what happened at Norwest.

The Norwest Company was a home building contractor known for superior-quality work. In the early years of the company, its focus on quality established it as a dominant contractor in the upper end of its market, and it prospered. When homeowners wanted the very best, they called on Norwest, and Norwest delivered.

The driving force behind Norwest was its young president and founder, Jonathan Norwest. When he sold the company after ten years, his only advice to his successor was to demand perfection. He probably meant this recommendation as an admonition to maintain the company's high quality. Unfortunately, buyer George Fintter took his words literally.

Fintter was obsessed with perfection, and he used Norwest as a vehicle to express it. He coined a slogan that he posted around the building and used in company advertising: "Perfection Is Routine at Norwest." Fintter then initiated policies to support this claim. Employees were penalized for any mistake that could be identified as their responsibility. Any error, even the slightest, had to be corrected the instant it was discovered. People worked overtime to correct even unimportant mistakes.

All correspondence from the company had to be "letter perfect." Every single letter had to be approved by a manager one level higher than the sender. In days before word processing was commonplace, typists frequently retyped a letter over and over again before "quality checkers" approved it for signature.

Through a tracking system that Fintter designed, progress toward perfection was calculated and graphically measured. Employees who either wouldn't or couldn't perform to Fintter's standards and do business his way were dismissed. Before long, the entire company was focused on achieving Fintter's definition of perfection. Norwest became sick rapidly. As one employee put it, "Norwest is more concerned with making everything perfect than with its work for its customers." As Norwest neared "perfection," costs increased dramatically. To compensate, Norwest raised its already high prices. Fintter claimed that the quest was worth it. He could go to his charts and show how the company was making measured progress toward perfection.

Strangely, as Norwest became "more perfect," product quality, as perceived by the customer, declined. Instances of required rework increased. Late deliveries, a rare occurrence in the past, became more frequent. The company began to lose its reputation for quality. Then it began to lose its customers. Six months later it was bankrupt.

Infected Organizations

Norwest's experience shows how the behavior patterns of an obsessive-compulsive manager can infect an entire organization. Once the infection becomes well-established, it takes on a life of its own. When that happens, the illness usually continues even if the sick manager leaves.

With obsessive compulsion firmly in place, these destructive tendencies crop up throughout the entire organization:

- Managers all the way down the line continually look over people's shoulders to catch mistakes.
- Employees learn not to take the initiative.
- No one is willing to take risks of any kind.
- Innovations cease because they are not valued.
- Decisions are agonizingly slow.

You can imagine what effect these tendencies have on morale, on the development of new products and new ideas, and on the organization's overall vigor. How will that company survive?

You may have noticed by now that this kind of micromanagement is much like that which often occurs in neurotic companies. Indeed, the behavior is the same, but the cure is different. If you try to use the overload principle (see Chapter 6) in an obsessive-compulsive organization, an infected manager will find a way to check each and every one of your details, regardless of time or cost.

One sure sign that an organization is obsessive-compulsive is its claim that it does not make mistakes. For this reason, we shudder when we hear terms like *zero defects*. It's okay to have zero defects as a goal, as long as everyone realizes that they're not really going to reach it, at least not in this lifetime. Being compulsive about anything, even excellence, is dangerous. The healthy organization recognizes this. While it may seek continual improvement in a wide variety of areas, it recognizes mistakes for what they are: a necessary part of getting things done.

Treating the Obsessive-Compulsive Organization

There are four treatments for the obsessive-compulsive organization. Which one you use depends on your level in the company. The first two are for those in positions of authority; the second two are for subordinates.

1. Empowerment
2. Deregulation
3. Charters
4. Rule breaking based on unique expertise

Empowering Your Managers

Often the organization's obsessive-compulsive behavior originates with the person at the top. If that's you, and you recognize it, you're in good shape, because this disease is easily treated and you have the authority to do it.

You will probably find that the managers of subunits have become infected with your obsessive compulsion. The way to break the hold of this illness is empowerment. Give those managers the power to run their own show.

Do this without looking over their shoulder. Avoid micromanaging the assignments you give. Tell the managers you're available if they need help; even then, give the help and get out of the way. Strive for high standards, but expect occasional failure as well as success. If you can't trust the managers you have, fire them and get people you can trust to do the job without close supervision.

Deregulating

Even if your organization's obsessive compulsion doesn't emanate from you, you still have the power, and the responsibility, to stop it. The illness may have grown slowly and insidiously for years, but it can be arrested with firm action on your part.

Take a hard, objective look at the directives, regulations, or procedures by which your organization lives—and then get rid of 75 percent of them. Or drop them completely. Deregulate as much as you can. The idea is to have much less for your organization to be obsessive-compulsive about.

At the same time, encourage your people to focus on accomplishment rather than risk avoidance. Promote the idea that some mistakes are good. This will take time, because if the organization is obsessive-compulsive, few will believe you mean it at first. However, you can speed the process along by allowing people to make mistakes, then congratulating them for it.

If congratulating mistakes sounds farfetched, you might consider taking a lesson from Thomas J. Watson, Jr., founder of IBM. A new vice-president reported to him after causing the company to lose $10 million. "I know why you sent for me," he told Watson. "You're going to fire me."

"Fire you!" exclaimed Watson. "Why in the world would I want to fire you? We just spent $10 million as part of your education."

Allyn and Bacon, a textbook publisher, was founded at the end of the Civil War by educators who loved books. By the early 1980s, the company's annual sales had reached $30 million. However, it had become an obsessive-compulsive organization run by managers who cared less for employees than for what they could squeeze out for the bottom line. According to one report, lower-level managers had to account even for pens and paper clips.[1] Many employees left, and those that remained unionized. Only after Bernard Krauss, former CEO of Esquire, bought the company did a cure begin. Although Allyn and Bacon has had other problems, Krauss successfully treated this one by deregulating the organization. He let employees do more of what they do best and less of counting paper clips.

Even if you are not the leader of an obsessive-compulsive organization, there are still things you can do to break the illness. But since this disorder usually comes from the top

1. Craig R. Hickman and Michael A. Silva, *Creating Excellence* (New York: New American Library, 1984), p. 61.

down, essentially what you must do is learn to manage your boss. Two techniques for doing this are getting your boss to agree to a charter and carefully skirting the rules from a base of recognized expertise.

Getting a Charter

A charter is essentially a written statement of work. It defines your responsibilities, and those of your supervisor, in a particular area, and it spells out, in black and white, exactly what your supervisor wants done.

A charter is different from a job description, which often is so general and so broad that it fails to provide much guidance on day-to-day responsibilities. A work charter specifies precisely what you can and cannot do, and it designates the parts of your job that your manager wants you to emphasize. It outlines your assignment in specific terms and defines the results your manager wants to see. That way, you both know what is expected.

This technique is used as a matter of course by professional management consultants at the beginning of each contract, and it is also used in the clinical practice of psychology. The psychologist clarifies the goals of the therapy with patients before the therapy begins. That way, the patients know where they are heading, and they feel more in control. This "charter" facilitates and is part of the treatment.

The U.S. Small Business Administration (SBA) currently sponsors an innovative program at many universities that matches small businesses needing advice with upper-division and graduate-level business students, who are supervised by their professors. In general, the student consultant teams were doing excellent work, but occasionally "clients" were unhappy. "The report I got from the students was fine," these businesses would say, "but it wasn't what I really wanted." Eventually SBA administrators found that the problem was a misunderstanding. The "consultants" thought the client wanted one thing, while the client thought it was going to get something else. The SBA solved the problem quickly with a written charter of work to be done, just like those used by professional consultants.

Noting the SBA success, we soon started recommending that managers in companies develop charters when taking on new tasks or significant new responsibilities. Then we discovered that this technique is especially effective in companies that are obsessive-compulsive. The written document can help to break the compulsion. It forces your manager to think critically about what he or she *really* wants done and thus to recognize the incongruity between worthwhile activities and obsessive nitpicking.

We thought we originated the work charter idea. We were wrong. In going over old lecture notes from Claremont Graduate School, we found that it was Peter Drucker again. Drucker suggested, back in 1976, that all new employee-employer relationships begin with this kind of charter. Did Drucker's charter concept come from his theory of "management by objectives," or was it the other way around? We're not certain. But we do know that those who have adopted this charter technique have succeeded in their work to a remarkable degree. True, it is an aspect of treatment, but this is one treatment that bosses love. We've also discovered that it doesn't make any difference whether you are a new employee just starting work or someone who has been around for a long time. You can sit down and draw up a charter with your boss at any time.

Breaking the Rules

Obsessive-compulsive organizations are easy to recognize: There are thousands of procedures and rules, both written and unwritten, governing how things are to be done so the organization will be perfect. Many of them are unnecessary, even counterproductive. If you ask someone why a particular rule exists, you seldom get an answer.

One way to treat this organization is by breaking some of those rules. Start with one that is rather insignificant, then move on to something larger. As others see that you are breaking rules without getting into trouble, they will be emboldened to do the same. And pretty soon the obsessive structure starts to crumble.

Let's be very clear about this: We are not talking about breaking rules just for the fun of it. Your underlying goal is to break the organization of its obsession by demonstrating the invalidity of rules that exist only for the sake of achieving perfection.

If you're the CEO, you automatically have the power to break rules. If you're not, this could be a very dangerous strategy. If your organization is very sick, or the rule is perceived as very important, you could get fired. The trick is to work yourself into a position where you are recognized as an expert in some area. Being an expert gives a unique type of power in any organization, and you can use that power to treat an obsessive-compulsive company.

The interesting thing is that anyone can be perceived as an expert in some area. The trick is to develop some specialty and be recognized for your expertise in it. An older, high-level manager will listen to, and frequently follow the advice of, a very young attorney who has recently been hired by the company. This is true because the young attorney, no matter how inexperienced, is perceived as an expert in the field of law.

It is important that your expertise be unique in your organization. Your special knowledge should not be exactly the same as anyone else's, especially not that of your boss. If you are of the same specialty as your boss, he or she is much less likely to defer to your knowledge. In that case, you need to develop a specialty within a specialty. For example, if you and your boss are both marketers, then you need to develop expertise in some subspecialty of marketing, such as distribution or research.

There is one final requirement. You must develop your expertise in an area that is important to your company. It would be foolish to become the recognized expert in international operations if your company has no foreign operations and no possibility for any in the future. So pick an area that is crucial to your organization's mission.

Becoming an expert is not as difficult as you might think. It doesn't depend solely on natural ability; after all, Einstein flunked mathematics in school. And it doesn't necessarily take a long time. At Xerox, new hire Lois Banks was considered an expert in selling office copiers with direct marketing techniques in about five months. She took home a six-figure income less than a year after graduating from college. Michael Porter at the Harvard Business School was barely thirty years old when he was acknowledged as a leading business strategist. Peter Drucker was recognized as an expert management consultant before he even knew what one was. The army had mobilized Drucker, then a young newspaper correspondent in his twenties, because of his familiarity with a number of European corporations. The colonel in charge of the project called Drucker in and told him he was to be a management consultant.

"What's that?" Drucker asked.

"Don't be impertinent," the colonel snapped.

"By which," Drucker later reported, "I knew he didn't know what one was either."[2]

If neither time nor natural ability is a primary factor in acquiring expertise, what is? We've found that it comes down to only three elements: knowledge, training, and practice. Knowledge is the cumulative body of information that is important in your area of specialty; it is usually acquired through "book learning." Training is the additional insight you get by applying the theoretical knowledge in real-life situations. And practice is the reinforcement of that knowledge through many repetitive applications.

You don't even need all three. Steve Jobs and Steve Wozniak, founders of Apple Computer, were both first-year college dropouts. But both had educated themselves about computers, and they put into practice what they had learned.

There is one more step. Having expertise is not enough; you must also be *perceived* as having it. If you were hired for

2. Story told to William A. Cohen at Claremont Graduate School, Claremont, California, September 1975.

your expertise, then fostering such a perception is unnecessary; you already have it. However, if you are only one of many in your specialty, if you developed your expertise while employed, or if it is outside the job specialty you were hired for, you probably have some additional work to do.

We recommend two high-profile methods for making others aware of your expertise: writing and speaking. You might have an aversion to them—many people do—but they are excellent ways to develop a reputation as an expert.

Your writing can take the form of technical papers or reports for senior management, or articles in journals recognized in your field. An economist we know, with only a bachelor's degree, was promoted to chief forecaster in only three years on the basis of trend reports that she wrote in her free time. A young engineer was named head of his section after an article of his appeared in a prestigious magazine.

In the same vein, you should create opportunities for public speaking. Prepare a short talk on your specialty, and aggressively search out audiences: groups inside your company, outside professional associations, fraternal and civic clubs, or local colleges in need of guest lecturers or seminar leaders.

Whatever method you use, don't be shy about your accomplishments. Once you have something in print or are scheduled to speak, share this information within your organization. Send a copy of the article or the announcement to your boss, and to your company's public relations department.

Summary

In organizations, an obsessive-compulsive illness most often shows up as an unreasonable demand for perfection. It stifles innovation and demoralizes creative workers.

Four treatments are available, and they are linked to your position in the organization. If you head up the organization, deregulate as much as possible. If you have an unwell subunit, empower its managers. Treating the organization from other positions and levels requires some form of managing your boss. Two ways to do this are drawing up work charters and rule breaking backed up by recognized expertise.

Chapter 10

The Aftereffects of Disaster— Post-Traumatic Stress

Not all troubles come from heaven.
—Old Yiddish proverb

It ain't over 'til it's over.
—Anonymous

In early 1992, a middle-aged Kuwait City engineer walked into his wife's place of employment at midday and asked to see her. Minutes later, he quietly surrendered. In the interim, he had shot his wife and her boss to death. Explained one witness, "It is the *mahjnoun*, the madness...it finally breaks your mind. Two years ago, this kind of killing never could have happened in Kuwait. Now we see it all the time."[1]

In psychological terms, Kuwait suffers from post-traumatic stress syndrome. We call it post-trauma for short. *Post-traumatic stress syndrome* is a relatively recent name for a phenomenon that psychologists have recognized for some time: the serious emotional disturbance that follows a traumatic experience,

1. Mark Fineman, "Post-Traumatic Stress Leads to Anxiety, Violence in Kuwait," *Los Angeles Times*, 10 August 1992, pp. A-1, A-14, A-15.

sometimes quite a bit after the event. In recent years we have seen it in Vietnam War veterans whose lives are crippled by painful memories of their wartime experiences; the reaction may be triggered at any time, even by something apparently innocent. We have seen it in prisoners of war who murder their spouses years later, in discharged employees who return to their workplace with shotguns, and in victims of natural disaster who commit suicide after an unfavorable insurance company report.

Organizations, too, suffer from post-traumatic stress disorder. Although the results are rarely characterized by violence, they can be extremely destructive to the organization's well-being.

Post-Trauma in Companies

What causes post-trauma? The post-traumatic organization suffers from the effects of a traumatic event. The event itself might be:

- A takeover
- Loss of a major contract
- A major reorganization
- The death of a senior executive
- An external event, such as a lawsuit against the company
- Forced recall of a major product

Note that this disorder is not the trauma per se. Many companies are severely traumatized and yet survive, almost without missing a beat. Others are not as lucky. For them, the trauma causes a post-traumatic stress response that lingers on and may flare up at any time. The difference lies in how the companies respond. Let us compare two well-known examples.

On the morning of September 30, 1982, a medical examiner in Chicago made a fateful analysis. Three Chicago-area residents had died from cyanide poisoning; the poison was traced to Tylenol capsules. Investigators quickly determined that Johnson & Johnson, the manufacturer, was not at fault;

the capsules had been tampered with after they had left the factory. To consumers, that made no difference. Even long-time users quickly switched to a "safe" brand. In just ten days, Tylenol's market share plummeted by over 87 percent.[2] Industry analysts, journalists, and marketing experts advised Johnson & Johnson to leave the market gracefully.

Wounded, part of the corporation exhibited the symptoms of post-trauma. Some in the company recommended taking a hard line: that it wasn't the company's fault, that even firearms manufacturers didn't get blamed for offenses committed with their products. This was the turning point. Had the company continued in this direction, it would have soon gone into full post-trauma. You probably wouldn't be able to purchase Tylenol at your local drugstore today.

However, corporate executives didn't waste any time. They started treatment at once. Johnson & Johnson accepted responsibility for the safety of the product and withdrew all capsules from the market. The company set progressive goals to reinstate the product with a protected packaging. It instituted actions internally to build cohesion and keep the company team together to solve the problem. It used good listening techniques with both employees and customers. So successful was this treatment that within a year, the brand recaptured 90 percent of its former market share.

Contrast this with what happened when Exxon's oil tanker *Valdez* struck the Bligh Reef along the Alaskan coast on March 24, 1989, ripping open its side and spilling 11 million gallons of oil into Prince William Sound. It was the largest oil spill in history, and it quickly sent Exxon crashing into post-trauma.

The company couldn't believe it had happened. How could a tanker run aground? It must be the captain's fault; hadn't he violated company policy? Or it was the rough weather. Exxon was a law-abiding company; how could it be responsible? Exxon's delays in taking action, its many blunders once it did decide to act, and its vacillation over accepting responsibility brought enormous negative publicity to the

2. "Tylenol Restaging Made Possible by Firm's Solid Research and Consumer Trust," *Marketing News*, 28 October 1983, p. 1.

company. Stock prices fell, and untold millions of dollars' worth of goodwill was lost. The cost in hard dollars was staggering: $2 million in cleanup costs, then $1.25 *billion* in damages as part of a settlement of federal criminal charges.

A year after the *Valdez* affair, Exxon had another spill, the result of a gash in its New York–New Jersey pipeline. Exxon reacted immediately and executed major cleanup efforts. The company was even congratulated by the Coast Guard and the manager of Clean Harbors, the organization that maintains the emergency equipment for cleanup efforts. However, recalling the *Valdez* affair, many still blamed Exxon.

The post-traumatic company is psychologically disoriented. In reaction to the stress, the organization may exhibit the following symptoms:

- Shock, erratic behavior, or both
- Overreference to a negative event in the past
- Actions that conflict with crucial needs

New Technology was a consulting company that provided corporations with training in marketing, management, and personal development. With the onset of a recession, New Technology's sales began to wane. At first it controlled its costs and maintained its profitability by reducing its seminars. Then, in one three-month period, it lost three major training contracts and had to cancel more than a dozen seminars because of inadequate enrollment. These developments cut its forecast sales in half.

In response to the trauma of losing so much so quickly, the company began acting erratically and without thinking. Most of the support staff were laid off. There weren't even enough people left to conduct the training already scheduled. Top management dismissed new ideas out of hand and avoided seeking new business for fear of additional losses.

Then the president, desperate for a positive cash flow, hired a vice-president who promised to rebuild the business rapidly through direct mail. This vice-president rehired staff people to run the direct mail program, but sales continued to fall. The remaining trainers were let go as the company struggled to avoid insolvency. The new vice-president was fired shortly before the company went under.

Companies struggling with post-trauma cannot perform at top capacity; sometimes performance is not even adequate. People may seem to be doing their jobs in a daze. Routine tasks may get done, but as soon as circumstances call for a deviation from standard operations, some kind of breakdown is likely. A common sign of this illness is overreaction to small emergencies that in healthier days would be fixed in a snap.

If the circumstances that led to the trauma involve a company shake-up, as they often do, the post-trauma will be complicated by the stress of the new situation. There is a new leader to get used to. Some employees may have left, voluntarily or otherwise. The survivors feel nervous, insecure, and guilty. Rumors are probably far more prevalent than in more normal days, and, true or not, they are all believed. People keep referring to events of the past.

This unstable and disoriented state leads organizations to take ill-considered actions that can cause serious damage. The wrong action may cause workers to be fired unjustly and unnecessarily. Even the correct action, inadequately thought through or poorly executed, may result in millions of dollars lost. For instance:

- A top executive moves a lower-level manager to a new position without considering the effect of this action.
- Someone launches a new product but fails to provide for promotional support. The product fails.
- A financial executive obtains needed funds for the coming year, but the timing is wrong and causes serious losses.

Erratic actions typify the post-traumatic company. If you see an organization taking actions that seem to make no sense, you should suspect post-trauma. Look at that company's past history; was there some traumatic event?

Consider the following erratic behaviors:

* In the early 1960s, the U.S. Air Force asked more than a thousand pilots to leave active duty. Almost the same day, it identified the need for two thousand more pilots for the following year.

* A division of a major accounting firm fired two highly specialized accountants the same week that it won a contract requiring the additional services of five such accountants.

* A manufacturing company liquidated its entire inventory of a household appliance at 50 percent of cost two weeks after it received a foreign order for 250,000 units, and thus the company could not fulfill the order.

These erratic actions could be traced back to some type of trauma:

* The Department of Defense had told the air force it faced major budget cuts, far and above what had been expected. Budget officers looked only at present-year operations; they didn't consider inventory planned for the following year.

* In the accounting firm, a senior vice-president had just calculated an unexpectedly high overhead.

* An unfavorable article in a respected business journal had called the household appliance obsolete.

Treating the Post-Traumatic Organization

We have found the following techniques helpful in treating post-trauma:

• Progressive goal setting
• Cohesion therapy
• Distraction therapy

Setting Progressive Goals

Progressive goal setting is a prime treatment for post-trauma. You can use it wherever you are in the organization. If you are a manager, start with your unit; if not, start with yourself. Focus on three short-term, worthwhile goals. If the trauma has been caused by an unexpected emergency, the goals should be aimed at resolving that problem. For example, if you were the executive that had been told to get rid of two accountants, you could set a goal of finding an alternative way of reducing budget. Select relatively easy goals that you can accomplish in a few days. List all the action steps you must take to reach each goal. Rank these according to importance and time sequence.

Now comes the most important step: Take the actions to reach your goals. Block time out of your day to fulfill the action steps; put them on your calendar. Allow yourself to work on nothing else during these periods. If you are a manager, insist that members of your organization follow the same rules.

As soon as you reach these goals, set three others. They should be slightly more difficult and longer-term; maybe these can be reached in a week or so. When these are done, pick three more. Repeat the process until you are working every day toward difficult, long-range goals. But be sure they are possible to achieve. This is not the time to set goals that no one but you thinks can be reached. The secret is to take action every day toward worthwhile organizational objectives.

Some call continual progression toward a worthwhile goal the central definition of success. Certainly the following examples support that view:

* In San Francisco, Richard Thalheimer almost lost his small company when a supplier failed to furnish him with a product that he had already advertised in a magazine. First he solved his immediate problem. He then treated his post-traumatic company through progressive goal setting. Today his company, The Sharper Image, has more than eighty retail stores, and mail-order sales run in the hundreds of millions of dollars.

* When his restaurant failed, Colonel Harland Sanders had to live on his social security. He hit on the idea of selling his family recipe for "Kentucky Fried Chicken" to a fast food restaurant. Achieving this "short term" goal took him three years and more than a thousand sales calls. But he took action every day, and that enabled him to reach this first goal. Then he moved on to sell his recipe to other establishments.

* P. F. Collier and Son started publishing books in 1885. At first Collier's books were sold only through bookstores. The company made six major attempts to sell books through the mail. All failed. In one case, the company spent $25,000 and sold just eighteen sets of books; that amount of money is like $1 million today. These company losses caused major post-trauma. In 1926, a nephew, Robert Collier, started treatment using progressive goal setting. He decided to try selling just one item through mail order; it would be a book on practical psychology called *The Secret of the Ages*. His first goal was simply to write and place the advertisement. At that point, the book didn't yet exist. (This type of dry testing is no longer legal, so don't try it.) When he got enough orders, he sat down and wrote the book. He then set higher and higher goals. In this way, he sold $1 million in books at $7.85 each in six months. The post-trauma disappeared. The book, by the way, acquired a life of its own. It is still in print and is selling today from the Robert Collier Book Corporation. The book has been selling through the mail continuously for almost seventy years!

Using Cohesion Therapy

Cohesion means sticking together. The idea is to get organization members to band together and stay together in the face of problems, whatever they are. Cohesion diminishes and fights post-trauma.

Much of the research on cohesion comes from military studies begun during World War II. S.L.A. Marshall, a military historian and battlefield psychologist, concluded that soldiers who knew each other and their leaders were far likelier to perform effectively than soldiers who were randomly assembled.[3] He also concluded that the main motivation for a soldier to fight was not patriotism, ideology, or even survival. Rather, it was a sense of psychological unity with other members of his organization. According to Marshall, "I hold it

3. Christopher C. Straub, *The Unit First* (Washington, D.C.: National Defense University Press, 1988), p. 6.

to be one of the simplest truths of war that the thing which enables an infantry soldier to keep going with his weapons is the near presence or the presumed presence of a comrade."[4]

More recent studies have corroborated this theory. A psychological study of jet bomber crews showed that time flown together was the most important factor in predicting crew performance. Another study showed that cohesiveness led to higher training scores. In cohesive units, more talented individuals voluntarily spent their free time teaching and coaching those less talented.[5]

Oddly enough, trauma itself can stimulate cohesion. That's like germs' stimulating the growth of antibodies that in turn attack the germs. However, traumatizing an organization deliberately is dangerous. And you don't need to do this. You can develop cohesion more easily in less dangerous ways.

To build cohesion, you must develop pride in group performance. That can be a challenge if the original trauma was caused by a failure to perform well. This difficulty is easily overcome. Find some other aspect in which the organization excels, and focus on that. In that one area, the organization can take pride in being the best.

For the purposes of building cohesion, exactly what you choose as "best" really isn't important. Many companies claim to produce the best product. Some organizations say they are the fastest, the most courteous, the most thorough, or the most creative. Some boast that they work the hardest, get the toughest assignments, or work the longest hours. We even know one company that promoted itself as the most fun-loving!

The point is to aggressively promote whatever it is that your group is the best at. You want each person to see constant reminders of the group's excellence. Gradually the feeling of pride in this one area will bring a mental shift away from the post-trauma.

How do you do the promotion? Use your imagination;

---

4. S. L. A. Marshall, *Men Against Fire* (New York: William Morrow, 1947), p. 42.

5. Jon W. Blades, *Rules for Leadership* (Washington, D.C.: National Defense University Press, 1986), pp. 76–78.

have fun. The possibilities are almost unlimited. Here are a few suggestions:

- Write a story for the company newsletter.
- Get yourself invited to give a talk to a local civic club; tell the story of your group's successes.
- Promote your group on a one-on-one basis every time you talk with someone.
- Think up a motto and have it printed on the organization's stationery.
- Have buttons or pins made up expressing the new theme, and present one to each member of the group.
- If your group has an athletic team, change the team's name to something that reflects the new focus.
- On Friday afternoon, invite the entire organization to a social hour hosted by your group; serve ice cream sundaes with "the world's richest chocolate sauce from the world's best accounting department."

One very positive point of this treatment is that it can be administered from any position within the organization. You can begin it at the top, at the bottom, or from any position in between. It is equally effective no matter where it begins.

Employing Distraction Therapy

With distraction therapy, you take some deliberate action to distract the organization from its post-traumatic condition.

Massive layoffs during the recent recession hit a division of one corporation very hard. We would have bet that the organization would fall into depression, but it didn't. Instead, it became post-traumatic. Its response was to refer back to the activities it was engaged in before the trauma, activities that in the new environment were no longer appropriate. A new vice-president tried to persuade the division to shift its activities toward the new reality, but he was only partially successful. For example, prior to the layoffs, divisional management was mostly engaged in deciding who would be laid off and who must be retained. Now that no further layoffs were planned, it was foolish to continue detailed personnel analysis. However, the organization had been so focused on this one activity for so long that it couldn't seem to quit.

The vice-president decided to use distraction therapy. He introduced a number of new projects simultaneously. These took a great deal of time and involved every department in the division. The organization was so busy that it didn't have time to think of past events, much less continue actions that were no longer appropriate. In fact, there were so many new projects that all of them couldn't be completed. The divisional vice-president knew this, but he insisted that they be done anyway. After some time, the divisional managers came to him and in strong terms asked him to reconsider. They presented an excellent analysis showing which projects should be done and which held in abeyance. The vice-president, with a quiet smile, allowed himself to be persuaded. All the projects to be completed were implemented without mishap. By then, the organization no longer was post-traumatic.

There are many ways of implementing distraction therapy, but the principle is always the same: to distract the organization out of its shock and overreference to past events. Here are some techniques you might consider:

- Put the organization to work on something that has nothing to do with its past problems. This is what the divisional vice-president did with his multiple new projects.
- Put the organization to work on a major effort that is the exact opposite of what is expected. For example, if your human resources organization has been concerned primarily with layoffs, get it to work on a major recruitment program.
- Put the organization to work on a major project that will have the effect of overcoming future problems. This use of distraction is a little riskier, because it may serve to remind organizational members of problems associated with the post-trauma. However, if the work keeps the organization busy enough, and if you use other techniques to maintain morale, this type of distraction therapy can work quite well.

Summary

Post-traumatic stress syndrome, or post-trauma for short, is the debilitating aftereffect of some traumatic experience; it may be felt some time after the original trauma, and it can be triggered at any time. An organization suffering a post-traumatic reaction will either go into something very much like shock or be subject to erratic actions that seem to work against sensible goals.

Three ways of treating post-trauma are:

1. Progressive goal setting
2. Cohesion therapy
3. Distraction therapy

With this chapter, we conclude the discussion of the nine psychological disorders that can affect organizations. In the next chapter, you learn how to accurately diagnose the situation in your organization.

Chapter 11

What's the Problem Here?— Diagnosing Your Organization's Illness

The beginning of health is to know the disease.
—*Miguel de Cervantes,* Don Quixote

I leave this rule for others when I'm dead. Be always sure you're right—then go ahead.

—*Davy Crockett*

Diagnosis is the starting point for treating any troubled organization. And it is critical that your diagnosis be accurate. The wrong medicine, no matter how powerful, won't help, and it can even make the situation worse. You must probe deeply to discover exactly what is wrong before beginning any intervention.

Author Stephen R. Covey tells this wonderful little anecdote to illustrate the importance of deciding on a diagnosis first:

> Suppose you've been having trouble with your eyes. Signs are just a blur. Even your television

viewing is unclear. Suspecting that you may need glasses, you decide to pay a visit to an optometrist.

You are welcomed into an office by a kindly gentleman wearing a white coat and glasses. Diplomas attesting to his education and other testimonials fill the walls of his office. He appears to be highly intelligent.

"What seems to be the trouble?" he asks.

"I no longer see very well," you answer. "Most signs are just a blur, and I can't see television clearly anymore."

"Aha!" he exclaims. "I think you need glasses."

Before you have a chance to reply, he takes his own glasses off and hands them to you. "I've worn these for years," he says. "I had the same problem. Now I see perfectly. You can keep these. This is my spare pair."

You hesitantly put the optometrist's glasses on. You see worse than you did previously. "These don't help," you tell him. "I see worse than before."

"That's strange," he says as he strokes his chin. "They work great for me. Maybe you aren't trying hard enough. Try to see harder."

"I'm trying as hard as I can," you insist. "I can't see a thing."

"Maybe you aren't thinking positively. Try that."

"I still can't see anything."

"Ah, I see the problem. You've got to improve your quality of sight. Take these glasses home with you and work on improving the quality of the way you see."

"That's stupid! I can't see well with these glasses."

"Boy, are you ungrateful!" he chides. "You don't want to see better."

How much confidence do you have in a doctor who prescribes before attempting to diagnose? Whether he or she is kind, well meaning, or highly qualified and intelligent is irrelevant. Yet, many corporate consultants routinely prescribe treatment with no diagnosis in the exact same manner.[1]

Using the Organizational Health Analyzer

Psychologists diagnose troubled individuals according to the symptoms of their illnesses. You can diagnose organizations in the same way. First you investigate what is wrong. You note the symptoms. Knowing what illness these symptoms represent, you can begin treatment.

Sounds simple, right? Well, normally in practice it's much more complicated. Sometimes the same symptom points to two different problems. Sometimes more than one problem is present at the same time. Sometimes exceptions in behavior cloud the picture. That's why, up to now, only trained psychologists with years of experience could treat companies using standard clinical techniques. Not anymore. We have designed a special diagnostic tool to help you find all the symptoms and correctly diagnose the problem. This tool, which we call the Organizational Health Analyzer (OHA), is a self-administered questionnaire. It is extremely simple and can be used successfully by anyone without special training in psychology. It shows you whether your organization is sick or well; if the organization is sick, the OHA pinpoints what it is suffering from.

Here's how it works: The OHA presents sixty-three statements about your organization and asks you to record the extent to which you agree with each one. On the answer key, your responses are converted to a numerical weighing that, when totaled, gives you nine separate "scores." Any individual score over 21 signals a possible area of trouble. Adding together the nine individual scores also gives you a quick way to measure the organization's overall health; a total of 180 points or more indicates that something is wrong, even if each

1. Based on an anecdote in Stephen R. Covey, *The 7 Habits of Highly Effective People* (New York: Simon & Schuster, 1989), p. 236.

individual score is in the "normal" range. The complete text of the OHA and the score sheet appear in Appendix A.

You may be surprised to find some problems in an organization that seems to be functioning quite well. This could be perfectly normal. Some psychological dysfunctions may be present without being disabling. Organizational disorders become a threat only when the symptoms are constant and severe.

What About Conflicting Symptoms?

Many symptoms you observe are common to more than one illness. Usually, this does not create problems in using the OHA because we already corrected for variances. However, if more than one illness is present, you may not get clear-cut results with the OHA. This may also be true if there are false symptoms or temporary symptoms. On the rare occasion when the OHA does not clearly distinguish between illnesses, you must do just what a psychologist would do: Use your common sense. Drawing on your familiarity with the organization, trust your gut feeling to determine which symptoms are real and which can be ignored.

Look at the severity of the symptoms as well as their persistence. Are they always present, or do they appear sporadically? Are they growing or fading? Eventually you will find that one ailment is far more likely. When that happens, your diagnosis is 90 percent complete. If sets of symptoms are about equal in strength and do not fade, note all illnesses that are present.

You can use Figure 1 as a quick cross-check. Note, for example, that the symptoms of neurotic behavior are self-doubt, paralysis, fear, anxiety, and inability to act. Maybe you recall several instances when you needed a decision to proceed, but senior managers sat on it until it was too late because they weren't sure which was the best decision. You look over the summary of symptoms in Figure 1 and see that self-doubt is also a symptom of intoxication. However, the other symptoms of intoxication don't seem to fit; they don't remind you of any specifics about your organization.

Figure 1. Symptom-diagnosis summary.

Ailment	Symptoms	Example
Manic behavior	Expansive moods, grandiosity, excitement, little attention to detail frequently leading to tragedy	A company forgetting important "details" in its rush to, and certainty of, success.
Manic-depression	"Roller coaster" of up-and-down mood swings	A company always chasing the next big contract. Results of manic-depression can be bizarre, such as hiring and firing of identical specialties simultaneously.
Schizophrenia	Disorganized structure, chaos, no clear lines of authority or responsibility	An organization that operates in a disorganized fashion and relies on luck for its success.
Paranoia	Lack of trust, strong emphasis on security, significant fear of outside intentions	A company refusing to let its own managers communicate with its customers without permission.
Neurotic behavior	Self-doubt, paralysis, fear, anxiety, inability to act	Montgomery Ward's forfeit of leadership to Sears after World War II.
Depression	Apathy; lack of energy, initiative, or commitment; guilt; desire to give up	A company facing layoffs because of lack or anticipated lack of business.
Intoxication	Inability to do self-analysis, addiction to source of intoxication, self-doubt, insecurity, rationalization	A company addicted to a self-defeating culture or philosophy, escaping facts through rationalization.

(continued)

Figure 1 (*continued*)

Ailment	Symptoms	Example
Obsessive compulsion	*Work never good enough, need for perfection, tendency to avoid or postpone decision making*	*Bosses demanding perfection in the search for "total quality."*
Post-trauma	*Shock, erratic behavior, overreference to events in the past*	*Company lays off its work force due to declining sales—yet it cannot gain sales without a work force.*

Who Should Take the Survey?

The OHA is a very simple tool that anyone can administer. So who should answer it? That depends largely on your position in the organization.

If you are in charge, you have a decision to make: Should you answer the questionnaire yourself, or should you also get others in the organization to take it? The advantage of having some of your staff do it, in addition to yourself, is that other points of view can be extremely revealing. A possible disadvantage is that sometimes the mere fact of being asked the question causes people to become aware of the issue, and then it becomes something of a self-fulfilling prophecy. This is a judgment that you as the leader must make. Think about the severity of the problem as it appears to you. Think about the size and makeup of the organization. Think about the personalities of the individuals whom you are considering for the OHA. Think about your own leadership style. And ask yourself how objective you think you can be.

If you are not in a position of authority, that is no reason for you not to do the OHA yourself. After you've finished the questionnaire, sit down with your supervisor, explain what you have learned about organizational illness from this book, and go over the results.

How Do You Interpret the Numbers?

It may happen that when you use the OHA to diagnose your organization, the results are unmistakably clear; the overall score definitely indicates a problem, and the individual scores tell you with certainty where it lies. But things are not always so simple.

Sometimes the general score is within the healthy range, but one or more individual areas are too high. For instance, suppose your scores are:

Manic behavior	18
Manic-depression	15
Schizophrenia	16
Paranoia	20
Neurotic behavior	34
Depression	16
Intoxication	24
Obsessive compulsion	13
Post-trauma	12
Total	168

The total reading does not indicate an illness, since it falls short of 180. However the neurotic behavior count is high; it's in the range we classify as "probably ill." You should also take note of the score for intoxication. It is not unusual that when one illness is present, some symptoms of other illnesses are also present. So you would probably proceed with diagnostic tests for the high counts just to be sure.

Sometimes you have the opposite problem: Total score is too high, but no one area stands out as the obvious problem. Suppose you took the OHA and came up with these scores:

Manic behavior	20
Manic-depression	21
Schizophrenia	20
Paranoia	19
Neurotic behavior	21
Depression	21

Intoxication	21
Obsessive compulsion	20
Post-trauma	18
Total	181

This reading shows a possible illness—the total exceeds 180—even though no one count falls within the danger range. Since the individual totals are so close together, it is difficult to diagnose the problem. Fortunately, this type of reading is infrequent.

Confirming the OHA Diagnosis

In both of the preceding examples, the results are less than crystal clear. The solution: Take steps to confirm the diagnosis. In fact, you should do this in every case. Diagnostic testing is especially important when the readings are close together, but we recommend that you *always* confirm the diagnosis before proceeding with treatment. The correct diagnosis is too important. Remember, no matter how much you want to help, the wrong medicine can hurt.

Diagnostic Tests: Procedures

In this section we describe several diagnostic tests for each illness. Select one or more and confirm your diagnosis before proceeding. If you cannot confirm your original diagnosis, return to the analysis stage and take another look at the organization. Check symptoms again; have some disappeared or changed? Redo the OHA based on your reevaluation. Repeat the procedure until you are reasonably certain of your diagnosis.

Manic Behavior

- Look for many errors on every project, with only slight concern for what might have happened or will happen.
- Make a slightly "off the wall" proposal. Look for immediate acceptance or an okay to proceed with little analy-

sis or for goals with insufficient resources to reach them. If the proposal is accepted, do not automatically proceed.
- Introduce a couple of straightforward proposals. Look for supervisors to immediately build them into grandiose projects far beyond your original intent.
- When you observe that a project hasn't been analyzed, propose several analyses. Note reluctance to look too closely into any project.

Manic-Depression

- Look for major changes in direction over a short period of time. Look for announcements of great success or opportunities followed by announcement of great problems, or vice versa.
- Make a beneficial suggestion. Look for outright rejection, followed by reconsidered total acceptance up to a few days later.
- Introduce two roughly equal suggestions several days apart. Look for expansive acceptance of one and arbitrary rejection of the other.
- Look for an overreaction when you make a minor error after having recently been congratulated for some accomplishment.

Schizophrenia

- Develop some simple but nonroutine plans. Attempt to implement. Look for problems that can be traced to lack of organization or to clear lines of responsibility or communication.
- Check for high personnel turnover.
- Check to see whether even simple projects regularly turn into chaos.
- Note whether you have difficulty locating the person responsible for a particular task or function.

Paranoia

- Do something that you don't normally do; for example, if you normally don't work over the weekend, do so, or

take sick leave if you usually don't. Then look for a
suspicious response.
- Ask questions outside of your normal area of responsibility. Look for a suspicious response.
- Ask colleagues about something out of the ordinary.
  Look for fear of management or established policies.
- Suggest that certain information be shared with another
  group in the company. Look for a lack of trust in which
  sharing, unless absolutely required, is considered the
  wrong thing to do.

Neurotic Behavior

- Make a beneficial suggestion. If it is rejected, watch the
  manner of rejection. Is it arbitrary rejection? Does the
  person you ask automatically turn to higher-level managers for approval?
- Note the time it takes the organization to react to changes
  in the environment. No reactions, or slow reactions, are
  indicative.
- Look for overreaction to problems or bad news.
- Make a proposal that requires some work in an area that
  the organization has not dealt with previously. Look for
  an overly negative response.
- Look for good plans, but poor execution.

Depression

- Check for frequently flagging commitment or widespread
  indifference.
- Make suggestions or recommendations. Look for unen-
  thusiastic acceptance or outright rejection from lack of
  power to implement.
- Take the initiative on something. Look for disapproval
  rather than approval from bosses, colleagues, and
  subordinates.
- Ask for something out of the ordinary. If no one has the
  power to do anything, suspect depression.
- Look for frequent nonprofessional behavior.

Intoxication

- Tactfully ask a question of a supervisor about a recent problem or failure. Don't press the issue, but look for a defensive attitude and excuses rather than reasons.
- Look for the same type of mistake repeated over and over again.
- Suggest a way to increase customer satisfaction. Look for a response that indicates the customers don't matter or that the company knows better than the customer.

Obsessive Compulsion

- Voluntarily accept responsibility in an area in which you have already proved yourself. Note whether your boss insists on looking over your shoulder, checking every action.
- Ask your boss for a decision that requires some important trade-offs. Note how long it takes this supervisor to make a decision. Difficulty with decision making tends to confirm obsessive-compulsive behavior.
- Look for a number of established routines that have little perceived benefit but are performed anyway.
- Look for work that is criticized "for lack of perfection" even though it is very successful. Be careful of this test, since with "total quality management" and allied approaches, managers are seeking continual improvement. You're looking for the attitude that *only* perfection is acceptable.

Post-Trauma

- Look for actions that contradict common sense, such as instructions to lay off employees despite approved plans, and without good reasons.
- Introduce a positive suggestion requiring action by one or more managers. Look for a bizarre or numbed response, as if the individual were in shock.
- Say "good morning" to people. Look for a dazed response, or no response at all.

Diagnostic Tests: An Example

Remember the example earlier in this chapter in which the neurotic behavior reading was high? In such a case, you might be tempted to check back through the chapter on that illness, pick a treatment you like, and blunder ahead. But don't. No matter what score you get, confirm the results before you do anything.

Look at the diagnostic tests just suggested for neurotic behavior. One is to make a beneficial suggestion and see how it is received. This doesn't need to be complex. Even a small suggestion, maybe something you've been thinking about for a while, can be used. Think up some suggestion that can clearly benefit the organization but requires a change in procedure—neurotics fear change.

Quantify the benefits and costs. Don't neglect risks, if there are any, but show why the risk is minimal and how you plan to handle it. Now, present your suggestion to your manger. If he or she doesn't have the power to approve it, ask that it be forwarded to a higher authority for a decision. If your suggestion is adopted, that's fine. You probably misinterpreted the symptoms. Go back and recheck the symptom list in Figure 1. There is no harm done, and you'll probably get a career boost for your efforts. If your proposal is considered but rejected, the organization may still be okay. Look closer at *how* the idea was rejected. Outright rejection, with little or no real consideration and transparently poor reasons given, is clearly neurotic. Your boss might even refuse to forward it, with a comment such as "I know they won't buy something like this."

You may think you are measuring your supervisor's aversion to change with this test. You're not. Someone who is aversive to change will give you more than enough excellent reasons for a rejection. But when the reasons given are half-baked or make no sense, that's neurotic. Similarly, if your boss doesn't even want your suggestion to go to someone who has the authority to order it done, then he's exhibiting the organizations' neurosis, not his own. When an organization becomes neurotic, that type of behavior permeates the entire organization.

Summary

Before you can start any treatment on an unwell organization, you must discover what is wrong. Even superb medicine can harm if given for the wrong illness. A simple tool for making a preliminary diagnosis is the Organizational Health Analyzer (OHA). Anyone can use it to find out the state of the organization's overall health as well as to identify the presence of certain likely illnesses. But the OHA results must be confirmed, and there are several tests that can be used to double-check the original diagnosis.

After confirming your diagnosis, refer back to the chapter on that illness. You will find additional information about the illness and different strategies for treating it. Now you have all the information you need to sit down and plan the treatment. We show you how to develop your treatment plan in Chapter 13. But there is one other thing you must do first.

Chapter 12

Protecting Yourself From the Sickness— The Sphere of Wellness

The preservation of health is a duty. Few seem conscious that there is such a thing as physical morality.

—Herbert Spencer, Education

Only those means of security are good, are certain, are lasting, that depend on yourself and your own vigor.

—Niccolò Machiavelli, The Prince

Sick organizations are not always rational. Just like a human patient, an organization suffering from a psychological ailment can hurt you even as you are trying to help it. To protect yourself, you must create around yourself a sphere of wellness, a protective circle that insulates and shields you from the craziness going on around you.

The sphere of wellness allows you to survive in a crazy organization. It buys you time while you go to work making things better. It also protects you, psychologically, when you begin talking about the problems to those above you in the organization. One very popular way to eradicate bad news is to shoot the messenger. So before you start a treatment plan,

use one of the following techniques to ensure your own
sanity, and keep yourself from getting shot.

Maintaining a Positive Outlook

Psychologists believe that you cannot be happy and unhappy
at the same time. If you think about this, it is really logical. If
you want to be happy, even in the face of misery about you, it
is within your grasp. You have the power to control your
mood.

For most people, just changing posture and facial expression can have a strong therapeutic effect. Try this. If you are
feeling down right now, sit or stand up straight, hold your
head high, put your shoulders back. Now smile. Paul Ekman,
professor of psychology at the University of California, found
that moods could be changed by simply assuming a happy or
a sad expression. Students that assumed a sad face felt sad;
those that put on a happy face felt happy.[1]

To top things off, try repeating this litany at the same
time: "I feel happy, I feel healthy, I feel terrific!" Keep saying
this loudly and with enthusiasm until you really feel it. W.
Clement Stone of Chicago developed this positive affirmation;
he claimed it helped him maintain a positive mood under
adversity.

Here's another experiment. Get yourself back into your
happy, smiling posture. If you have nothing to smile about
right now, think of a time when you did; perhaps you achieved
success or received some very good news. Assume the same
posture, facial expressions, and feelings you had when you
were happy and successful in the past. Now, maintaining the
facial expressions and posture of happiness, *try* to get depressed. Try to feel really bad. Unless you change your posture, expressions, and thoughts, it just isn't possible.

You may be interested to know that nature has a sound

1. David Lewis, *The Secret Language of Success* (New York: Carroll & Graf
Publishers, Inc., 1989), p. 68.

explanation for this phenomenon. When we frown, certain muscles tighten to compress small blood vessels from the carotid artery; smiling activates other muscles that open up blood vessels. Thus, these actions regulate the flow of blood, with its mood-altering chemicals, to the brain. Psychologist R. B. Zajonc at the University of Michigan believes nature may have intended that people control their emotions in this way.[2]

In this simple truth—you can't feel bad when you feel good—you have a very powerful way to make yourself feel good whenever you wish. Conjure up a happy thought from the past, assume the same posture and facial expressions, and you've got it! Even if the atmosphere around you is negative, you are able to keep yourself in a positive frame of mind. That positive outlook is a major dimension of your sphere of wellness.

Handling Problems

Success at solving problems contributes greatly to your sphere of wellness. You can increase your problem-solving skill with a technique developed by researchers at Duke University. It's actually a form of self-hypnosis.

First, select the major problem bothering you. Go off by yourself where it is quiet. Sit down and allow yourself to relax, with your eyes closed. Most people find they can get into a fully relaxed state by slowly imagining a numbness spreading over their bodies, from their toes to their head, even including their eyelids. In this relaxed state, describe the problem to yourself and tell your subconscious mind that you want the problem solved. Then get up and go about your business. Sooner or later, the solution will come to you. Sometimes the results are immediate. Sometimes the problem is solved a little later, with the solution appearing in different or unexpected ways. We know this sounds too good and too simple to be true. But it has been tested and found to work.

2. Ibid., p. 67.

Using the Body's Chemical System

You can also build and maintain a sphere of wellness by using your body's own chemical system. Norman Cousins explained in his book *Anatomy of an Illness* how he cured a life-threatening illness through his own body's chemistry. He theorized that the human body contains its own drugs that can promote the physiological and psychological changes necessary to cure any disease. These chemicals are released through specific psychological or physical stimulations that we do not yet fully understand.

Among the most powerful of these drugs are the endorphins. Strenuous exercise can release endorphins, a fact that probably explains the euphoria frequently experienced by joggers toward the end of a workout and known as a "runner's high." Maintaining a consistent exercise regime is one way of ensuring that endorphins are in your bloodstream on a regular basis.

However, exercise isn't the only way. Cousins was able to release endorphins while on his "deathbed" by watching Three Stooges movies nonstop. At first, the going was tough. He found that six hours of belly laughs would release sufficient endorphins to allow him fifteen minutes of sleep. Slowly, the drugs worked their magic, and eventually he was able to get the sleep he needed for recovery.

In seminars we have helped train thousands of executives in how to release endorphins by this simple exercise. We ask them to stand, close their eyes, and allow their minds and bodies to relax. We then ask them to imagine that when they return home that evening, they will find among their mail a registered letter from an attorney, notifying them that a wealthy uncle has passed away and left $1 million tax-free, which is enclosed. The only condition is that they must spend this money in any way they wish. They can buy a home or an expensive car, take a trip around the world, or give the money to charity. Anything they want.

We give the executives several minutes to imagine their good fortune and the wonderful things they could do with this tax-free money. We then tell them that on the count of three, they are to open their eyes. They then have ten seconds to tell two other executives what they've decided to do with the money. They are to do this in the most excited way they can.

You can actually feel the excitement building as we slowly count, "One . . . two . . . *three!*" The room breaks out into a loud babble of noise. After ten seconds we stop them—which is not always easy—and invite them to feel the endorphins coursing through their veins. All agree that they feel fantastic.

You can do the same exercise by yourself. You don't have to continue imagining that a rich uncle leaves you a million dollars; that can get a little old after a while. Instead, pick your own dream. Sit back and daydream. Imagine you have achieved one or more of your dreams, whatever they are: financial or personal, job-related or not. Picture what your life would be like. See yourself enjoying your success. Really give yourself a squirt of endorphins. Dose yourself with a "dream session" daily. You will surely maintain your sphere of wellness, but you may get more. Many people tell us they eventually achieve what they think about while releasing endorphins in this way.

Reframing

Yet another technique for maintaining a sphere of wellness is called reframing. Basically, what you do is look for advantages in any disadvantageous situation. Whenever the company, in its sickness, presents you with a difficult circumstance, try looking at it a different, more positive way.

Suppose, for example, you're the press relations specialist in a government agency that has become obsessive-compulsive. Your immediate supervisor continually returns your press releases, pointing up minor errors and insisting they be re-done. You take issue with these instructions. Some of what you're told to change isn't really incorrect, in your opinion. Besides, the reworking takes up precious time; if press releases aren't timely, they're worthless. But you have been given specific instructions.

You have a choice: You can make yourself crazy telling yourself how weird everything is around here, or you can find another way to look at it. Can you see this as a challenge to your ingenuity? Can you come up with a suggestion that would assuage your boss while still allowing you to get releases out on time, such as investing in new software or getting the summer intern to help with proofreading? Can you make room for the possibility that indeed you might occasionally make mistakes, and your supervisor's attitude is forcing you to be more careful?

Creating Mind Movies

This last technique for building a sphere of wellness is one of our favorites. It works best in situations where those around you behave in very bizarre ways and, in the process, cause you to feel very upset emotionally. For example:

- Your supervisor makes unreasonable demands, scolding you in demeaning ways.
- A new project is beset with errors and communications mix-ups; it looks like something the Marx brothers would do, and you're getting blamed.
- The entire organization is so depressed that the illness is all anyone can talk about; everywhere you turn, you get reminded how awful things are.

Whenever it seems you are in danger of getting sucked into emotionally harmful situations, take time out for a mind movie. Be especially watchful if you think your organization is depressed, post-traumatic, or neurotic.

To create your mind movie, sit down alone in a place where you won't be disturbed. In your mind, re-create the event or situation that is upsetting you. If it's an actual event or sequence of events, review the action as it actually happened. If you're upset by the possibility of what *could* happen, review an imaginary sequence of actions, your worst nightmare. At first, this mind movie may be painful to watch, but don't worry. You will soon change that.

After viewing your mind movie once, play it backward. That is, see everything happening in reverse: people walking backward, steam getting sucked into a pot, water flowing upward and back into a glass from which it was spilled, and so on. You may remember those old movies in school that were sometimes erroneously run in reverse. That's what you want to see. Does this look a little ridiculous? Good. That's exactly what you want.

Now play the mind movie forward again but increase the speed, faster and still faster. Now slow it down into slow motion. See the figures moving and speaking in slow motion. Speed them up again. Make them look as ridiculous as you can.

Now add some sound effects. Change the voice quality of the villains in the event so that they sound strange, but not threatening. Give them squeaky voices like Mickey Mouse or quacky voices like Donald Duck. Hear your boss yelling at you in Tweety Bird's chirping tones. If the voice is normally pitched low, change it to a high pitch. If it is normally a high female voice, change it to a bass pitch. Change the tone of voices to make them sound frightened, nervous, or sleepy. Any change that makes your mind movie funny and ridiculous is a good change.

Now let's use some other special effects. Change the villains' appearances. Have them grow long noses, pointed ears, long tails, or big rears. Make them look as foolish as possible. Shrink their size so that they are very tiny.

Now change the events. Have the characters behave in any way you want. You can have them make an apology—or congratulate you. Or maybe you just have them say foolish things. Keep playing the movie backward and forward while you are doing this. Vary the speed, the color, and all of the other elements.

It's time for the final touch: a little music. However, make the music totally inappropriate: a little circus music for a "serious" financial discussion, or a cartoon theme song for the staff meeting. You're the director of this mind movie, so it's up to you. You can do anything you want.

Keep watching your mind movie of the distressing event until it is no longer stressful. Keep watching it and adding special effects until you have to stop yourself from laughing out loud. In fact, this is the only drawback. In the future, when someone mentions or discusses this formerly distressing event, you may have to work hard to keep yourself from smiling.

Summary

Building a sphere of wellness around yourself can help you stay healthy even while the organization is sick. If you build successfully, the symptoms of the organization's illness cannot harm you. In effect, this buys you time while you treat the illness.

Techniques for creating your own sphere of wellness include:

- Maintaining a positive outlook
- Solving problems through self-hypnosis
- Using the body's endorphins to create positive energy
- Reframing the stressful situation
- Creating mind movies

Chapter 13

A Plan for Treating the Disease

A plan is nothing; planning is everything.
—*Dwight Eisenhower on commanding the Allied invasion of Europe during World War II*

You've got to be very careful if you don't know where you are going, because you might not get there.

—*Yogi Berra*

There is an old saying that those who fail to plan, plan to fail. Once you have made and confirmed your diagnosis, it is very tempting to jump right in and start treatment without a plan. You may think you "don't have time to plan." Others may say, "Oh well, the plan is in my head." These are just excuses.

You must resist the temptation to plunge ahead. A formal, structured treatment plan is a vital and necessary step in treating psychologically ill companies. Not only will you save much time and effort over the treatment period, but a formal plan can provide you with the most effective and efficient way of achieving wellness. It alerts you to pitfalls in your plan of attack. It helps you weigh the advantages and disadvantages of one approach over another. Documenting your thinking in a plan helps you create combinations, permutations, and sequences in your treatment that you might otherwise miss.

Writing down your planned treatment actions in a plan helps you to maintain course as you proceed.

Treatments rarely go exactly as planned. That's okay. Most processes with complex, difficult goals run into unexpected factors that cause deviations from what was planned. Our moon-bound astronauts aimed for a target 240,000 miles away. They were off course most of the time. But because they had a plan, they were able to continually correct their course to reach their goal. You're in the same situation. Unexpected factors will cause deviations as you carry out your treatment. If you don't have a written plan, it is easy to lose sight of where you are heading when circumstances force you off your planned course.

Psychologists and planners have also discovered that formalizing your treatment plan has other advantages:

- It forces you to think ahead.
- It allows you to coordinate different efforts going on at the same time.
- It helps you to develop definitions and standards so you can measure improvement and know when you have reached your goal.
- You are better prepared for change.
- You have more control over the treatment.
- You are able to make better use of the resources you have.
- You gain a clear awareness of problems, opportunities, and threats.

Developing the Basic Concept of Treatment

No doubt you recall from earlier chapters that each of the nine disorders has several possible treatment techniques. You may also remember that occasionally organizations suffer from more than one illness simultaneously. Therefore, developing a treatment plan is not simply a matter of picking one treatment out of the hat and writing up a time line. You may end up using several different specific treatments; you may administer them simultaneously, or one at a time. You might use one sequence of treatments in one situation and the same set of treatments in another sequence in a different situation.

That is why we speak of "treatment concept" rather than individual treatments. The treatment concept is your overall prescription for bringing the organization back to health.

How should you go about it? In this chapter, you learn the steps in the process; in the next chapter, you have a chance to watch the process in action, in a real-life business setting.

The approach we recommend for developing a concept of treatment is used in several professions. In business, it is sometimes called the Harvard case study method. It is also used to analyze cases in the legal profession. The same approach is used for analyzing psychological problems and developing a course of treatment in clinical psychology. Strangely, the method was originally developed for use by the U.S. Army General Staff in the 1890s; in fact, it is still used by the armed forces for staff studies today. The fact that this device is used by so many different professions is evidence of its flexibility. It also confirms the device's value for getting at the heart of a problem and determining the best means to solve it.

The process involves five steps:

1. Review the diagnosis.
2. Define all relevant factors.
3. Determine possible alternative concepts; list advantages and disadvantages of each.
4. Analyze alternative concepts.
5. Choose the most appropriate.

Let's look at each of these steps in turn.

Diagnosis

Correct diagnosis is the most important task you can accomplish in treating an organization. With an accurate diagnosis, even a less than optimal treatment can still work. But if you misidentify the illness, even a brilliant treatment may cause the organization to grow worse instead of better. Always have in mind that the diagnosis is the foundation of the treatment plan.

Relevant Factors

The task at this stage is to scan the total environment and note all the factors that are relevant. Factors are all the elements that exist in the situation. Notice we don't refer to "facts." Facts are very important. But you must also be aware of theories, assumptions, estimates, definitions, criteria, and scenarios with varying degrees of accuracy. If you fail to recognize them for what they are, you may inadvertently treat them as if they were facts. In doing so, you may well overlook some important dynamics.

But not all factors are truly relevant. If you attempt to list every single factor that you see, you will become lost in detail and suffer informational overload. Therefore, you must take the time to weigh each factor to determine whether it is relevant to the organization's disease and potential treatment. If it bears on the disease or treatment, it's relevant, and you should include it. If it doesn't, leave it off your list.

Alternative Concepts

As with most things in life, there's more than one way to go about treating a dysfunctional organization. In this stage, you list all the treatment concepts that seem possible and sensible. Start by reviewing the techniques suggested in the earlier chapters on the individual illnesses. Visualize various combinations of techniques. Then, take your list of options and write down the advantages and disadvantages of each one. Take your time with this; think each one through carefully.

Analysis of Alternatives

This is the core of the development process. Each of the possible alternatives that you listed in step three is thoroughly

defined and tested against the relevant factors that you identified in step two. This involves weighing and evaluating the
relative importance of the advantages and disadvantages of
each alternative. The disadvantages of one course of action
may be unimportant when measured against criteria in your
relevant factors. A particular treatment concept could have
advantages that relate to one very important factor. You are
documenting a logical thought process that funnels your thinking toward a single concept of treatment.

A good way to proceed with this analysis is to take each
treatment concept and show how it fares against relevant
factors. This may reveal new pros and cons. As you proceed,
additional relevant factors may occur to you. If so, go back
and add them to your list. Then consider the list of alternative
concepts again. Do the new factors change anything? Can you
think of other alternatives, or additional advantages or disadvantages to a treatment concept you've already listed?

At the end of this step, you should be able to choose the
one best concept of treatment. If you are unable to narrow
your alternatives to a single choice, show why the best alternatives are about equal.

When we do an analysis, we sometimes test our conclusion by showing the first four steps to someone who under-
stands this process but is not familiar with the specific case.
We leave off the last part, where we choose a single treatment
alternative. We ask which alternative that person would pick
and why. Usually when that person selects a different treatment concept, it is due to one of two reasons. Either we made
use of assumptions or knowledge that we did not note in our
relevant factors, or we missed something. If we discover new
insights or holes in our logic, we modify our plan.

The Final Decision

In this final step, you record your conclusion. This is a
summary statement of the final result of your analysis in step
four. Here you clearly spell out the precise concept of treatment you intend to follow. If you think of something you

missed, go back to the relevant step and rethink it. Then go through the succeeding steps to make sure your change doesn't affect something else further down the line.

Developing the Treatment Plan

Although you now know the basic concept of treatment, you do not yet have a treatment plan. You know *what* you are going to do but not *how*. The treatment plan outlines the *how* and much more. It is a formal document that you use throughout the treatment process to keep yourself on course.

We recommend the following outline for your written plan:

1. Diagnosis and situational analysis
2. Problems, threats, opportunities
3. Concept of treatment
4. Metrics
5. Management and implementation

Diagnosis and Situational Analysis

In this section of your plan, present the diagnosis of the illness and how you arrived at it. Describe the situation and the environment. Include all the relevant factors you have identified and anything else that helps you describe what you found.

Problems, Threats, Opportunities

In this section, you summarize elements from the previous section that you consider critical problems, threats, and opportunities. Your goal is to show how your concept of treatment will solve the problems, avoid the threats, and take advantage of the opportunities. For example, a cash flow crunch might be a major problem. A competitor's new invention could be a major threat. A forecast of growing demand for your kind of product over the next two years might be the basis of an opportunity.

Concept of Treatment

Here you record the treatment concept you have already chosen after analyzing all the alternatives. You have already done the thinking; this stage is where you commit the plan to writing.

> "Would you tell me, please, which way I ought to go from here?" asked Alice.
> "That depends a good deal on where you want to get to," said the cat.
> "I don't much care where," said Alice.
> "Then it doesn't matter which way you go," said the cat.
>   —Lewis Carroll, *Alice's Adventures in Wonderland*

Metrics

How will you know when the organization is "cured" of its illness? That's what metrics are for. They spell out specific benchmarks and criteria. When you achieve them, you know your job is done. Without metrics, you haven't got a treatment plan—you have a collection of facts, concepts, and ideas. They may be interesting. They may do some good. However, they won't be enough to help you return the organization to a condition of wellness.

You can establish metrics in terms of sales, profits, market share, personnel turnover, customer satisfaction surveys, measurements of quality—whatever fits your situation. Make them as specific as you can. They should state clearly what you expect to happen and when. That way, you can measure your progress as your proceed.

Your metrics should concern only that part of the organization you are treating. If you are a first-line manager, your metrics should concern your group, not the entire corporation. But if possible, design your metrics so they are linked with the basic purposes of your organization. That way you advance the organization in its basic mission as you help your unit get well.

Beware, however, of using the wrong metric. Many years ago, as a young lieutenant in the air force, I arrived at my first base and went to the officer's club. On the wall was an impressive plaque: "Presented to the Best Officer's Club in 2nd Air Force." I soon discovered, to my surprise, that the club did not come close to measuring up to its award; I found the food awful and the waitresses surly. One aspect that particularly irritated me was that there were no catsup bottles; catsup came in little plastic containers, like those in aircrew flight lunches.

I eventually learned that the "Best Officer's Club in 2nd Air Force" was the club that showed the best profits, not the one that gave the best service. To cut expenses, some enterprising soul had developed a system of collecting the unused catsup and mustard packets from the flight kitchen. Since flight crews had already paid for them, the officer's club got them for nothing. Free catsup equals lower expenses equals increased profit.

When not flying, I prefer my catsup from a bottle. I started bringing my own bottle to the club. Several months later, our new base commander happened to be dining several tables away from me. A waitress suddenly appeared at my table and reached for my catsup bottle, explaining that the colonel needed it. I told her that this was my personal catsup bottle and that the colonel couldn't have it. This caused such a look of consternation on her face that I partially relented. I told her that the colonel could *borrow* my catsup bottle, on one condition. She must explain to the colonel that this was a loan, and that this officer's club didn't supply catsup bottles. The base commander listened attentively to her explanation, then nodded toward me. From then on, I didn't need to bring my catsup bottle to the club. Starting the next day, catsup bottles sprang up like mushrooms on every table.

In considering this incident in recent years, I believe it is not only a classic case of the wrong metric, but an excellent example of correct treatment.

Management and Implementation

This is where you get very specific. Figure out exactly what actions you need to take, and in what sequence. You have to consider how much time each action will require, who will be directly involved in it, and who might be indirectly involved. Consider all the ramifications: What other elements will be affected if the action isn't completed as scheduled? All these details need to be thought through and spelled out in the plan.

To help with this stage, we developed a tool that we call the Treatment Schedule (TS). The TS lays out the actions you will take and when you will take them. You also include the metrics points that measure progress. In effect, it is a "how goes it" tool that you can continually refer to during the entire treatment process.

Figure 2 shows the basic format of the TS. On the left side, write in actions and metrics. Across the top, put the time periods. We usually recommend time periods of one week. Once you start treatment, you can write in the actual dates.

Triangles represent benchmarks, the dates when actions are supposed to start or finish. If an action involves a span of time, two triangles are connected by a horizontal line. When an action is completed, shade in the triangle to make it solid. If the action is completed sooner than expected, draw a new triangle and shade it in. If the completion date has to be postponed, draw in a new triangle at the appropriate spot; when that action is completed, shade in the triangle. If you need to adjust dates again, draw in new triangles.

Let's go through Figure 2 together. The specific actions aren't important at the moment; just look at how the times—planned and actual—are represented.

Action 1 was started on time, but completion was several days late. So a new triangle was drawn and shaded in for the actual completion date. This made action 2 late also, so again

Figure 2.   Sample treatment schedule.

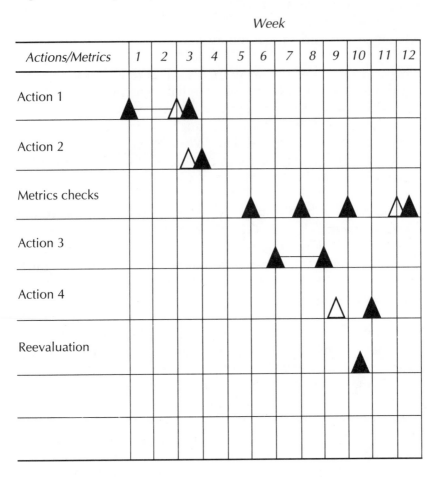

a new triangle was drawn and shaded in. Metrics checks were scheduled every two weeks; all but the last were done on time. Action 3 was started and completed on time, but action 4 was over a week late. The reevaluation was conducted on time.

If you change or modify your treatment along the way, you can make the necessary adjustments right on the TS. If the treatment is changed substantially, prepare a new TS.

You may recognize the TS as a form of Gantt chart. As with a Gantt chart, you can also include money factors in the

TS. If you sum the cost vertically, you can monitor the cost of treatment weekly. If you sum horizontally, you get the total cost for each action.

Accounting for New Factors

It is impossible to anticipate every new event in the life of a sick patient. That's true whether the patient is a human being or an organization. Sometimes changes mean new opportunities for ending problems much sooner than you thought, or in a way that wasn't possible before. At other times, new events may set your timetable back or require you to change treatments. As important situational variables change, you should revisit your plan and adjust as needed.

No treatment plan should be set in stone. Keep an open mind. You should be continually scanning the environment, monitoring your "patient" and observing results. Sometimes results are very fast, almost instantaneous. Other times, it takes a little longer.

If there is no improvement at all in a reasonable amount of time, say a month, reevaluate your treatment plan. You may need to change the sequence, alter some aspect of the concept, or try something altogether different. When one treatment isn't effective for a particular illness, another will be. As with any illness, sometimes one strategy works better than others, and some won't work at all. That's normal.

If new symptoms appear, of if the symptoms change, revisit your diagnosis. Like the practice of medicine or clinical psychology, treatment of organizational disorders is as much art as it is science. Don't get discouraged. Your skill and judgment in managing the treatment while faced with a multitude of sometimes conflicting variables will increase with experience.

Summary

Once you have completed your diagnosis and confirmed it, it is essential that you take the time to develop a written treatment plan outlining exactly what you intend to do. The first step in the planning process is to develop the treatment concept, which involves investigating the environment for relevant factors, listing possible alternative concepts with their advantages and disadvantages, analyzing those alternatives, and choosing the one best option.

With the treatment concept, you know what you are going to do. The written plan specifies how you will do it, with benchmarks to measure progress along the way.

As you implement your plan, continually monitor progress; if results are not what you intended, or if new variables arise, adjust your plan.

Chapter 14

A Success Story

*Take time to deliberate, but when the time for action has arrived,
stop thinking and go in.*

—Napoleon Bonaparte

Know what thou canst work at.
—Thomas Carlyle,
Scottish essayist

Don Severn had been with a major aerospace company for
twelve years when he was named marketing vice-president
for his division. At first, Don resisted the promotion. His
roots were in developmental engineering, in which he held an
advanced degree. As a project director, he had developed a
major weapons system valued at hundreds of millions of
dollars. He told the president that he would prefer to wait
until an engineering vice-presidency became available.

When he finally became convinced it was the right move,
Don jumped in with both feet. As vice-president of marketing, he would be responsible for the marketing managers,
including their selection, training, and assignment, and for all
new business activity, including bidding on competitive contracts. In addition, he was the senior adviser to the president
on marketing issues. His department consisted of twelve
marketing managers plus a small staff of researchers and
clerical and administrative personnel.

Don worked hard at learning his new job. He attended

many marketing seminars and took evening courses in marketing at a local college. He listened carefully to his staff and avoided snap decisions. Eventually, he won the trust and respect of his staff and the confidence of senior management. His department was credited with being an important factor in winning several major contracts with the U.S. government. In the space of only five years, many came to regard him as something of a marketing expert.

But Don was becoming increasingly concerned about his department. Divisional sales had declined for the past two years. While some of this was due to the general downturn in defense business, his win-loss ratio on the contracts he bid had also declined from almost 35 percent in good years to 12 percent. He was also losing more of the high-dollar bids. He assigned some staff members to a competitive analysis. What they learned was very troubling: While industry sales overall were declining because of cuts in the defense budget, their division was doing much worse than the competitors. Don's key managers thought the problem was that they were pricing their services too high.

Don didn't waste any time. He hired consultants skilled in bidding proposals to work with his department and the key engineers involved in marketing efforts. These consultants felt that price was not the main issue. They instructed Don's staff and others on some aspects of bidding that had not been given much attention before. While this effort resulted in better proposals, improvements in win-loss ratio were only marginal. The consultants thought that the situation would improve over time.

Don wasn't so sure. He was still losing too many bids. To add to his concern, the president had charged him with leading the effort to locate new markets. Don feared that the new effort would turn up even more problems that he didn't yet know about. He wanted to get everything cleaned up. Don had heard of the concept of treating organizations with clinical methods, and he began to wonder if his department could be suffering from a psychological malady.

He sat down to review what he knew about himself and the department. As an engineering manager, Don had made decisions mostly by himself. When he got into marketing, he knew he'd need to change. He did a complete turnabout to a much more participative style, and it worked! Now, most of the major decisions were made jointly by him and his marketing managers. He was proud that with almost no controls, his organization enthusiastically took on every job.

Don did, however, realize that sometimes his staff bid contracts he felt were too difficult; he also noted that they were overconfident about winning such contracts. Sometimes it felt as if they were on a roller coaster. They would start off enthusiastic, with high expectations of winning a particular contract; then they would bid and lose. Everyone would feel pretty bad for a while. But when another opportunity came along, everyone would pitch in, and before you knew it, work was at a feverish pace again.

If Don had had more experience as a corporate therapist, he might have been considering manic-depression at this point. But even experienced therapists move cautiously, and that's exactly what Don did.

Diagnosing the Problem

Don decided to take the Organizational Health Analyzer. His results were borderline:

Manic behavior	17
Manic-depression	26
Schizophrenia	20
Paranoia	16
Neurotic behavior	20
Depression	20
Intoxication	25
Obsessive compulsion	18
Post-trauma	18
Total	180

The total of 180 is right on the border between normal and unwell; we usually consider that a total score of 180 or above suggests a possible illness. But two specific areas were worth looking at; both manic-depression and intoxication fell inside the range of "possible illness."

Then he asked nine members of the department to take the OHA. Their totals were remarkably consistent, and Don made this composite:

Manic behavior	21
Manic-depression	31
Schizophrenia	21
Paranoia	18
Neurotic behavior	21
Depression	21
Intoxication	22
Obsessive compulsion	21
Post-trauma	20
Total	196

If anything, members of Don's department thought the problem more severe than he did. Don decided on a tentative diagnosis: manic-depression.

Confirming the Diagnosis

Don realized it was important to be sure of his diagnosis, so he set out to confirm his suspicions. He took an engineer's approach. First he pulled out all the communications to and from his office for the previous two years and copies of the division's internal newspaper for the same period. He then reviewed all these files, looking for a pattern. He found thirty-two memos announcing pending success or positive expectations. Some had to do with projects. Others described reorganizations or new work concepts that the department had adopted. He found fourteen of his own memos discussing various types of problems, and announcements of going-away luncheons for marketing managers. Don plotted a time line of all these activities and realized that they showed a pattern of success, or high expectations of success, followed by some sort of failure. That repeated cycle of elation and depression made it clear: The division was afflicted with manic-depression.

Developing the Treatment Concept

Relevant Factors

Next, Don sat down with a big yellow pad and developed the following list of relevant factors:

- Divisional sales have declined for the past two years. Part of this is due to an industry decline in government sales.
- Win-loss ratio on all contracts bid is declining.
- We are losing more of the high-potential, more important contracts.
- Our division is doing significantly worse than our competitors.
- With help from consultants we have better proposals but the win-loss ratio hasn't significantly improved.
- We make major decisions as a team. This probably explains the high commitment to projects despite considerable failure.
- Although manic-depression is the most likely culprit, the OHA also showed a somewhat high score for intoxication.
- We tried two reorganizations, but they didn't work too well, so I dropped them.
- Six marketing managers gone in two years is pretty high turnover.
- Since winning a bid involves many other elements besides the proposal (including contact with the customer, internal attitudes and relationships, and so on), the illness could be working elsewhere to affect bid results.
- Senior management seems to have confidence in me.
- Our company and our division are currently financially secure.
- If left untreated, the illness is likely to affect other areas of performance in the future as we move to develop new markets.

When he wrote down this last item, Don paused to think. Were there other symptoms of the manic-depression besides win-loss ratio? Aside from bidding on contracts, were there other areas where an up-and-down emotional cycle showed up? He came up with two.

He thought about that team he had put together to look at opportunities for new markets. At first the team members would get tremendously charged up about a particular opportunity, but whenever they ran into some negative data, they would actually get depressed before dropping it. It was almost funny. He actually had to help pull them out of their depression before they went on to look at the next opportunity.

The other situation was even funnier. The department staff had a Friday night bowling group that competed against other departments. They had never done particularly well; it was just something they did for fun. Recently, though, they seemed to be taking this activity more seriously. When they won, that's all they talked about Monday morning. When they lost, they acted as if it were a major factor in their lives.

Were these important factors? Maybe. He added them to the list.

Alternative Treatment Concepts

The basic idea in treating manic-depression is to get control. You need to apply structure, discipline, and strict controls. Don developed the following list of possible treatments, with advantages and disadvantages for each.

Alternative 1. Send the organization back to school to take relevant courses until the win-loss ratio improves.

Advantages

1. Going to "proposal school" did result in better proposals. Additional schooling in other subjects might lead to more improvement.
2. Additional schooling is a low risk to my current leadership style.
3. Additional schooling could be worked into current scheduling easily, so it would not be disruptive to the department.

Disadvantages

1. Previous schooling on proposals improved the proposals but hasn't improved the win-loss ratio significantly.
2. If the significant schooling didn't help, it could deepen the depression part of the cycle.
3. Even if successful, such schooling would only attack symptoms in one area.

Alternative 2. Change my style of management. Make all major decisions myself, using a more directive leadership style, as I did when I was an engineering manager.

Advantages

1. I have used this style successfully before, so it would not be totally new. Also, I've changed styles successfully before, so I know I can do it.
2. A directive style would give me total control. I could direct which contracts would be bid and which would not, and I could limit expectations and the mania part of the cycle through direct methods.
3. I now have the marketing expertise I lacked at first. It was this lack that initially drove me to a participatory style.

Disadvantages

1. A major change in leadership style is major surgery. Suddenly shutting down a participatory style is likely to cause major problems with everyone.
2. When I changed style previously, it was with an entirely new organization; now that my subordinates all know me, it may not be so easy.

Alternative 3. Institute standard operating procedures to gain control where my style of participatory leadership doesn't do this.

Advantages

1. Standard methods of operating will not materially affect my participatory style of leadership.

2. I can use the team approach to establish these formal methods or rules.

Disadvantages

1. Too much reliance on standard operating procedures could stifle accomplishment and creativity.
2. There could be some disciplinary problems with new policies.

Analysis of Alternatives

Now Don worked his way through the three alternatives, analyzing them as fully as he could. He decided that additional schooling (alternative 1) wasn't likely to help. There was no evidence that the department didn't know how to turn out a good proposal, bid contracts, or market. The schooling it had already gone through contributed little to bettering the win-loss ratio of bids. Additional schooling on other topics was unlikely to improve the win-loss ratio. Also, he realized the win-loss ratio was just a symptom of the disease. Schooling was unlikely to provide the control needed. So while that treatment would be easy to implement, it probably wouldn't be successful.

Completely changing leadership style (alternative 2) is no small thing. Suddenly going to a fully participatory style from a fully directive style or vice versa is very dangerous. Don felt it was likely that with a directive, authoritarian style he could actually bring the manic-depression under control, especially since he himself is not manic-depressive. However, there was considerable risk that the sudden change could cause the organization other serious psychological problems. Don decided to reserve this as a treatment of last resort.

There would be some risks in establishing formal operating procedures (alternative 3), but they were minimal, especially since everyone was aware that the department had problems. Also, Don could establish the new procedures using his participatory style of making decisions. That way, the department would be very committed to those controls.

Don was pretty sure the department could come up with procedures that would eventually improve the circumstances triggering the depression and the mania. But if this alternative were to fail, he could move to a more drastic treatment, such as changing his leadership to a more directive style.

The Final Decision

Don had reached his conclusion: The treatment concept would be a two-step approach. He would establish formal controls in all areas of the department's operations and try that for six months; if there was no significant improvement, he would add a second treatment—more directive management.

Developing the Treatment Plan

Now Don knew what he was going to do. His next step was to define how. To do that, he wrote a treatment plan.

Diagnosis and Situational Analysis

Here Don summarized the entire situation. He recorded what he had observed, the diagnosis he had made, and what he planned to do.

Problems, Threats, Opportunities

Don identified two key problems and threats:

1. The aerospace industry is depressed and is faced with declining sales with its traditional customers. In this environment a healthy company is critical to competing successfully.
2. Although, at the moment, symptoms of the illness are only evident in the area of bidding and proposals, other areas may be affected, either now or in the future.

He also noted two opportunities:

1. Since my supervisors seem to have confidence in me, and since the company and the division are in good shape financially, we have some slack time for treatment.
2. Our participatory team structure is well-established, so we can use this to help us set up treatment.

Metrics

Don decided he had a ready-made metric in his win-loss ratio. If the ratio improved, he would know the department's health was improving too. He knew it was important to be as concrete as possible, so he set some tentative numbers. In three months, he wanted to see the ratio at 16 percent; in six months, 25 percent.

Then, remembering that he had spotted roller coaster symptoms in other areas besides the bidding process, Don, the ultimate engineer, decided to stretch into the unfamiliar world of emotion. He felt it would be valuable to track changes in people's emotional intensity to see if the bounce from highs to lows would moderate as treatment progressed.

So he enlisted the aid of a human resources specialist in his company, and together they developed a brief opinion survey to measure emotional intensity. Everyone in the department took the survey after significant events. For instance, every Monday morning the bowling team had to answer this question:

How do you feel about winning (losing) Friday's match?

——Extremely depressed   ——Elated

——Very depressed   ——Very elated

——Depressed   ——Extremely elated

——Neutral

Of course, he was careful to explain to everyone what he was trying to do so that his measurements didn't cause other problems.

Don was less certain in this area, but with the help of his in-house consultant, he established improvement goals using his metrics as guidelines. He wanted to see less extreme values that would tend to cluster about the neutral description.

Management and Implementation

Now, to work out the specifics of the treatment plan, Don called on his best asset: his team. The team members met in their regular staff room, with the tools and processes they had used so successfully in the past to plan marketing campaigns for the division, and went to work on planning their own future.

The first area they turned to was the bidding process. They were charged with establishing some kind of policy that would disallow bids where there was little chance of winning. They decided to set up specific criteria, using hard numbers; if any project fell below these minimum criteria, they wouldn't bid on it.

They went about deriving these criteria very scientifically, analyzing data from past bids won and lost. They determined an optimum number of face-to-face contacts with prospective clients, and they even put numbers on the quality of those contacts. If any proposal situation didn't permit the minimum number of high-quality contacts, they didn't bid. They also figured out a way to classify proposals according to difficulty; if any potential proposal didn't met the minimum "doability" number, they would not bid. Once these and other controls were in place, they stopped getting manic about bidding every long-shot possibility that came along, and they stopped getting depressed over losing out.

At the same time, using pretty much the same process, Don had his new venture group develop criteria for the opportunities it was investigating. Like the controls team, this group quantified these criteria into go/no-go numbers that made it easy to decide which opportunities to pursue and which to pass up. This action forced the group members to look at every situation more realistically. In fact, they ended up reinstating some projects they had earlier abandoned.

One of the first tasks for both planning teams was to set up a timetable. How long would it take them to develop their controls? They set up start and completion dates, then worked out their implementation time line. With Don's help, they added in the metrics at checkpoints—they decided on two-week checkups—and a reevaluation date. Then they put the timetable in writing in their treatment schedule (see Figure 3).

Figure 3.   Marketing division's treatment schedule.
Date August 20, 1995
Diagnosis Manic-depression

Week

Actions/Metrics	1	2	3	4	5	6	7	8	9	10	11	12
Develop bidding controls	△	—	△									
Implement bidding controls			△									
Metrics checks					△		△		△			
Develop new market controls						△	—	△				
Implement new market controls									△			
Reevaluation: Modify treatment if required										△		

Results

The marketing department responded rapidly to Don's treatment. In just two weeks, the "emotion" surveys showed that the intensity of highs and lows was starting to ease off; the first tally showed a dip of 5.5 percent. The change in win-loss ratio was first apparent on smaller bids, since they tend to occur more frequently, but the results were more than anyone could have hoped for. In three months, the ratio improved to 21 percent. Even on larger contracts, where the bidding process is longer, the ratio started to show noticeable improvement in the fourth month. At each two-week checkpoint, the surveys showed that the amplitude of elation before bidding and depression after getting the results was continuing to lessen.

Don's department is doing well now. It's fit and competitive. Whatever the future holds, Don knows his team is ready.

Summary

In this chapter we have watched a manager on the firing line treat a disorder that was hurting productivity and threatening to cause even more damage in the future. Using a disciplined approach and a structured planning process, he diagnosed and then confirmed the illness, analyzed alternatives for treatment, selected the best one, and worked out a scheme for implementing treatment and measuring progress along the way.

Our final suggestions to you are to be flexible and innovative in your corporate therapy. You have some interesting challenges and tremendously fulfilling successes ahead.

Appendix A

Organizational Health Analyzer

Instructions: Circle the description that best represents your opinion of the following statements as they apply to your organization.

> *SD* = *strongly disagree*
> *D* = *disagree*
> *U* = *undecided*
> *A* = *agree*
> *SA* = *strongly agree*

---

1. Many managers doubt their own ability. They can't make up their minds without an okay from higher up.

   SD D U A SA

2. Goals and objectives seem inflated and divorced from reality.

   SD D U A SA

3. One day we are told that we are having the best year ever, the next that we are in trouble. Then the cycle repeats.

   SD D U A SA

4. No one seems to care about anything.

   SD D U A SA

5. Everything is always in a disorganized mess.

   SD D U A SA

6. Whenever people point out
   problems, others deny that they
   exist.   SD D U A SA

7. No one trusts anyone else.   SD D U A SA

8. My work never seems good   SD D U A SA
   enough for my boss.

9. Everyone seems in shock.   SD D U A SA

10. People don't seem to know   SD D U A SA
    what to do.

11. The attitude seems to be "Don't   SD D U A SA
    confuse me with the facts; don't
    bother me with details."

12. One day I'm a hero; the next they   SD D U A SA
    tell me I can't do anything right.

13. No one seems to have the energy   SD D U A SA
    to do anything.

14. Absolute chaos! No one knows   SD D U A SA
    what's going to happen next.

15. People repeat the same actions   SD D U A SA
    again and again, even though
    they don't work. These people
    rationalize why they don't
    do something different.

16. Everyone seems afraid of   SD D U A SA
    management's policies.

17. My boss keeps looking over   SD D U A SA
    my shoulder and checking and
    rechecking my work.

18. Managers behave erratically as if   SD D U A SA
    in shock.

19. The organization just doesn't seem   SD D U A SA
    able to know what action to take.

20. People are so excited that they   SD D U A SA
    aren't careful what they are doing.

21. We never know what to expect: SD D U A SA
    The organization is on either a
    real high or a real low.

22. No one is committed around   SD D U A SA
    here.

23. We have no real planning or organization in this company. SD D U A SA

24. There is an attitude that we know more than any expert, including our customers. SD D U A SA

25. In this organization, you can't trust anyone. SD D U A SA

26. The attitude around here is not to accept anything less than perfection. SD D U A SA

27. People seem spaced-out and don't react, as if they don't want to be reminded of their experiences. SD D U A SA

28. People seek approval from higher-ups too often, apparently out of fear. SD D U A SA

29. People are so strongly focused on outcomes that they overlook important details. SD D U A SA

30. One day we're told to do one thing; a couple of days later we're told the exact opposite. SD D U A SA

31. Little gains real commitment. SD D U A SA

32. We don't know who is in charge; we're disorganized. SD D U A SA

33. People are insecure. They hide their problems and make excuses. SD D U A SA

34. Everyone is overly suspicious about everything. SD D U A SA

35. It takes forever to get a decision because the decision maker wants things to be "just right." SD D U A SA

36. A simple event can trigger strange reactions: People respond as if in shock or paralyzed. SD D U A SA

37. There is a lot of worry about things that aren't important. SD D U A SA

38. Higher management will accept   SD   D   U   A   SA
    any kind of crazy proposal with
    very little analysis.

39. People are congratulated for a   SD   D   U   A   SA
    job well done; a couple of weeks
    later they are fired.

40. Even terrific ideas are received   SD   D   U   A   SA
    with very little interest.

41. Even simple problems seem to   SD   D   U   A   SA
    become chaotic.

42. We don't seem to learn our   SD   D   U   A   SA
    lessons. We fail to analyze our
    mistakes, so we end up repeating
    them.

43. People are scared silly that "Big   SD   D   U   A   SA
    Brother" is watching them.

44. We've got required routines   SD   D   U   A   SA
    that everyone knows add no
    value at all.

45. People sometimes appear shocked   SD   D   U   A   SA
    at something that is familiar.

46. We have good plans, but we   SD   D   U   A   SA
    can't seem to execute them.

47. Someone will introduce a simple   SD   D   U   A   SA
    proposal, and it will get built
    into a grandiose scheme.

48. It's impossible to keep track   SD   D   U   A   SA
    of management's opinion of how
    we're doing: It seems to go up
    and down.

49. No one shows any initiative   SD   D   U   A   SA
    around here; everyone lacks
    energy.

50. I have difficulty in finding out   SD   D   U   A   SA
    who is responsible for anything.

51. The attitude toward customer   SD   D   U   A   SA
    complaints is that our customer
    just doesn't understand the
    problem.

52. People are reluctant to share   SD   D   U   A   SA
information with other units
in the company.

53. People do great work, but they   SD   D   U   A   SA
are still criticized because it isn't
perfect.

54. When something happens, people   SD   D   U   A   SA
react strangely.

55. People doubt their own ability   SD   D   U   A   SA
to produce, and they fear taking
action.

56. The organization has unrealistic   SD   D   U   A   SA
goals.

57. One day there's elation, the next   SD   D   U   A   SA
despair.

58. Lots of people are indifferent to   SD   D   U   A   SA
what happens.

59. We have one crazy event after   SD   D   U   A   SA
the other.

60. People lose their objective   SD   D   U   A   SA
easily and tend to rationalize a lot.

61. There is above-average turnover in   SD   D   U   A   SA
employees.

62. The organization won't accept   SD   D   U   A   SA
failure; everything needs to be
perfect.

63. Certain things are sure to bring on   SD   D   U   A   SA
an overreaction.

Scoring the Organizational Health Analyzer

Instructions: Transfer your responses to this score sheet. Add across the rows horizontally to get the total for each illness. The highest total is the most probable illness. The higher the count, the greater the probable strength. For any single illness, use the following scale:

21 or less	=	normal
22–28	=	possible illness
29 or greater	=	probable illness

Next, add the total count for all illnesses. A total of 180 or more may indicate possible illness even if no single illness has an abnormal reading.

Mania

Statement	SD	D	U	A	SA	Total
2	1	2	3	4	5	_____
11	1	2	3	4	5	_____
20	1	2	3	4	5	_____
29	1	2	3	4	5	_____
38	1	2	3	4	5	_____
47	1	2	3	4	5	_____
56	1	2	3	4	5	_____
					M =	_____

Manic-Depression

Statement	SD	D	U	A	SA	Total
3	1	2	3	4	5	_____
12	1	2	3	4	5	_____
21	1	2	3	4	5	_____
30	1	2	3	4	5	_____
39	1	2	3	4	5	_____
48	1	2	3	4	5	_____
57	1	2	3	4	5	_____
					M-D =	_____

Schizophrenia

Statement	SD	D	U	A	SA	Total
5	1	2	3	4	5	_____
14	1	2	3	4	5	_____
23	1	2	3	4	5	_____

Intoxication

Statement	SD	D	U	A	SA	Total
32	1	2	3	4	5	_____
41	1	2	3	4	5	_____
50	1	2	3	4	5	_____
59	1	2	3	4	5	_____
					S =	_____

Paranoia

Statement	SD	D	U	A	SA	Total
7	1	2	3	4	5	_____
16	1	2	3	4	5	_____
25	1	2	3	4	5	_____
34	1	2	3	4	5	_____
43	1	2	3	4	5	_____
52	1	2	3	4	5	_____
61	1	2	3	4	5	_____
					P =	_____

Neurotic Behavior

Statement	SD	D	U	A	SA	Total
1	1	2	3	4	5	_____
10	1	2	3	4	5	_____
19	1	2	3	4	5	_____
28	1	2	3	4	5	_____
37	1	2	3	4	5	_____
46	1	2	3	4	5	_____
55	1	2	3	4	5	_____
					N =	_____

Depression

Statement	SD	D	U	A	SA	Total
4	1	2	3	4	5	_____
13	1	2	3	4	5	_____
22	1	2	3	4	5	_____
31	1	2	3	4	5	_____
40	1	2	3	4	5	_____
49	1	2	3	4	5	_____
58	1	2	3	4	5	_____
					D =	_____

Intoxication

Statement	SD	D	U	A	SA	Total
6	1	2	3	4	5	_____
15	1	2	3	4	5	_____
24	1	2	3	4	5	_____
33	1	2	3	4	5	_____
42	1	2	3	4	5	_____
51	1	2	3	4	5	_____
60	1	2	3	4	5	_____
					I =	_____

Obsessive Compulsion

Statement	SD	D	U	A	SA	Total
8	1	2	3	4	5	_____
17	1	2	3	4	5	_____
26	1	2	3	4	5	_____
35	1	2	3	4	5	_____
44	1	2	3	4	5	_____
53	1	2	3	4	5	_____
62	1	2	3	4	5	_____
					O-C =	_____

Post-Trauma

Statement	SD	D	U	A	SA	Total
9	1	2	3	4	5	_____
18	1	2	3	4	5	_____
27	1	2	3	4	5	_____
36	1	2	3	4	5	_____
45	1	2	3	4	5	_____
54	1	2	3	4	5	_____
63	1	2	3	4	5	_____
					P-T =	_____

M _____ + M-D _____ + S _____ + P _____ + N _____ + D _____ + I _____
+ O-C _____ + P-T _____ =

Total reading = _____

Appendix B

Summary of Symptoms and Treatments

Illness	Symptoms	Treatment
Manic behavior	Expansive moods, grandiosity, excitement, little attention to detail frequently leading to tragedy	Contract Plan Anchoring techniques
Manic-depression	"Roller coaster" of up-and-down mood swings	Discipline Focus on purpose Directive management
Schizophrenia	Disorganized structure, chaos, no clear lines of authority or responsibility	Control over mission/objectives Focus on center of gravity Ensuring that actions support mission Restructuring
Paranoia	Lack of trust, strong emphasis on security, significant fear of outside intentions	Trust Rule of reciprocity Reality confrontation Redirection
Neurotic behavior	Self-doubt, paralysis, fear, anxiety, inability to act	Involvement therapy using overload Reframing Social pressure Refocusing

Illness	*Symptoms*	*Treatment*
Depression	Apathy, lack of energy, initiative, or commitment; guilt; desire to give up	Distracting and refocusing Giving something to feel good about Winning a victory
Intoxication	Inability to do self-analysis, addiction to source of intoxication, self-doubt, insecurity, rationalization	Confrontation after rapport Past-present-future therapy Impact therapy
Obsessive compulsion	Work never good enough, need for perfection, tendency to avoid or postpone decision making	Empowerment Deregulation Charter Rule breaking
Post-trauma	Shock, erratic behavior, overreference to events in the past	Progressive goal setting Cohesion therapy Distraction therapy

Index

About the Authors

William A. Cohen, Ph.D., is a professor of business and institute director at California State University, Los Angeles, and the author of 28 business books. He has been a senior corporate manager and a consultant to government, Fortune 500 companies, and small businesses. His books include *The Art of the Leader, How to Make It Big as a Consultant, Building a Mail Order Business, The Entrepreneur and Small Business Problem Solver,* and *Developing a Winning Marketing Plan.* His textbook, *The Practice of Marketing Management,* has been adopted by 177 universities.

Bill Cohen holds a B.S. from the United States Military Academy at West Point, an M.B.A. from the University of Chicago, and an M.A. and Ph.D. in management from Claremont Graduate School. He is also a distinguished graduate of the Industrial College of the Armed Forces and a brigadier general in the U.S. Air Force Reserve.

Nurit Cohen, Ph.D., is both a clinical and an organizational psychologist. She has worked, taught, and consulted on problems in management, organizational development, and personal development in the United States, Israel, and Thailand. In addition to maintaining an active practice in clinical psychology, Dr. Cohen is chief executive officer of the consulting firm Global Associates.

Nurit Cohen earned a B.A. and M.A. in organizational psychology from California State University, Los Angeles, and an M.A. and Ph.D. in clinical psychology from the California School of Professional Psychology. She is a member of the American Psychological Association and the California State Psychological Association, among other professional organizations.

For many years, the Cohens have shared a professional relationship in addition to a marital one. Together, they offer consulting, seminars, and research services to industry and government organizations. They are co-authors of the book *Top Executive Performance*, which has been translated into five languages. Their work on "sick" organizations and the use of psychological therapies began in 1986. Realizing that traditional psychoanalytic methods were impractical in business applications, they turned to cognitive/behavioral therapy, a style of therapy that is much faster and more useful for helping troubled businesses. Their ideas, which have been tested and proven valuable for their clients, led to this book.

Bill and Nurit Cohen live in Pasadena, California.

—